THE HERMITAGE

A STROLL AROUND THE HALLS AND GALLERIES

AN ILLUSTRATED GUIDE-BOOK

P-2 Art Publishers

ST PETERSBURG

Foreword by Mikhail Piotrovksy

Introduction by Vladimir Matveyev

Text and compilation by Sergei Vesnin, Sophia Kudriavtseva, Tatiana Pashkova

English translation by Paul Williams

Designed by Nikolai Kutovoy

Colour correction by Liubov Kornilova

Computer type-setting by Yelena Morozova

Photographs by Darya Bobrova, Leonid Bogdanov, Pavel Demidov, Alexander Gronsky,

Sergei Falin, Leonard Kheifets, Victor Savik, Georgy Shablovsky, Vladimir Terebenin, Oleg Trubsky

Edited by Maria Lyzhenkova

Managing Editor Nina Grishina

ISBN 5-900530-74-4

STROLLING THROUGH THE HERMITAGE

The name of our museum comes from the French and means "a place of solitude". The times when it was the Tsar's private museum are long past, yet even today the Hermitage with its millions of visitors each year is one of the few places where it is possible to find solitude in a dialogue with world culture and Russian history. It is more than just contact with the sublime taking us away from everyday concerns: the Hermitage has its own special atmosphere that awakens the finest elements in the human spirit.

In the Hermitage you can breathe in different cultures, be fascinated by their distinctive features. You can admire masterpieces that stand above all national and cultural differences. You can reflect on episodes in Russian history, many of which took place, at least in part, within these walls.

The Hermitage is to a large extent a unique museum precisely because the history of the world embodied in its cultural attainments is here fascinatingly interwoven with the spirit of our own, Russian history. The ghosts of great artists, famous and anonymous, wander the halls of the Hermitage together with the shades of tsars and courtiers, soldiers and diplomats, writers and revolutionaries, who have left a living memory of themselves here for ever. The museum is so huge and the impressions it generates so varied that it takes many visits to get to know it. Strolling through the Hermitage is probably the greatest pleasure it offers us: to pass unhurriedly from hall to hall, from the historical state rooms to the masterpieces of Ancient sculpture or Dutch painting, thinking as you go about Matisse or Napoleon, Rembrandt or Stolypin, and, inevitably, about Catherine, whose will and taste brought the museum into being. Such a stroll is always full of surprises, even for those who know the Hermitage well. Your eye is suddenly caught by an elaborately carved chair you never noticed before. The sun falling in a different way gives a new vision of a familiar painting. You wander into one of the many temporary exhibitions held in the Hermitage. On the other hand, if works have been removed for exhibition elsewhere, their place might be taken by others from the museum stores. The Hermitage is inexhaustible and generous to those who love it. You can come here with a specific aim, or just to wander wherever the fancy takes you. In the Hermitage you can be constantly gazing from side to side or lost in your own thoughts. You can view the paintings and statues, but equally you can admire the floors and ceilings. You can make your way slowly, taking in every detail, or quickly, eager to reach some favourite, familiar spot. Yet there are few spectacles in the world more attractive than the views from the Hermitage windows: the Neva with the Peter and Paul Fortress and the Spit of Vasilyevsky Island, Palace Square, the Admiralty... The Hermitage entices, fascinates, charms. It never disappoints anyone.

The Hermitage is an extensive museum with many layers to it. It has everything: both spiritual enrichment and new knowledge for any visitor — child, teenager, preoccupied adult, and thoughtful pensioner. The museum is as welcoming to refined intellectuals and inexperienced provincials as it is to venerable scholars, to those still studying and discovering the world and those who are certain they have penetrated its deepest secrets. The Hermitage is equally open to all. Although an aristocrat and a snob, the Hermitage is the most democratic of museums, one where everyone finds something for his or her self.

The Hermitage has lived a very long and complicated existence. It has experienced wars and revolutions, fires, thefts, sales, neglect and lack of understanding. It has also known the emotional uplift of construction and the gambles involved in collecting, the pleasure and pride of saving something, self-sacrificing love and fanatical adoration. Losses and gains, failures and achievements — all of them are to be found in the life of the Hermitage today as well.

For more than 200 years the museum has carried out its sacred duty to be the guardian and curator of world culture on Russian soil. The Hermitage has itself become one of the most characteristic features of the Russian cultural tradition — its universality fused with uniqueness.

It always has something to say to those who visit, no matter how many times they have been.

Welcome to the Hermitage.

Mikhail Piotrovsky
Director of the Hermitage

←←
View of the Winter Palace
from Palace Square

←
Winter Palace. The Boudoir

New Hermitage
The Raphael Loggias

→
Winter Palace
The Malachite Room

The Hermitage is among the greatest museums in the world. Its fame is founded in equal measure on the majestic architectural ensemble, the outstanding collections of objects of art and culture from around the world, and an extremely rich past which is bound up with the foundation, rise and decline of the main imperial residence in St Petersburg. These three facets determine the museum's outstanding significance for Russian and world culture.

The Hermitage owes its origins to the creative and educational activities of the Russian rulers. The winter residence of the Russian monarchs became the centre around which a great museum, its architectural complex and its countless artistic treasures crystallised.

The successive Winter Palaces of Peter the Great, which stood on the site now occupied by the Hermitage buildings, established the pattern of constructing palaces on the main embankment of the new capital. Empress Anna Ioannovna, who reinstated St Petersburg as the capital in 1732, preferred the luxurious mansion of the late Admiral-General Fiodor Apraxin that stood a short distance away, by the Admiralty, but she decided not to break with tradition and move her residence from the bank of the Neva. On her orders a new riverside wing was built onto Apraxin's mansion and this determined the location of the residence for the future. In the years 1754–62, commissioned by Empress Elizabeth, Rastrelli created on the same site the Winter Palace that we see today. Catherine the Great, who took the imperial throne in 1762, immediately set about changing the layout and decoration of the rooms in the Winter Palace. It was her idea to construct the Small and Old Hermitages alongside the official residence to house her growing art collections. Between 1764 and 1787, on the Empress's orders, the Small Hermitage and then the Large (Old) Hermitage were constructed along the embankment, while the Raphael Loggias block was built onto the latter along the Winter Canal. This was followed in 1783–87 by the construction, a little further up the Neva, of the Hermitage Theatre, linked to the Old Hermitage by an arched aerial walkway. In Catherine II's enlightened age, then, a whole group of buildings appeared by the Winter Palace that became known by the general name of "the Hermitage".

The last element was added to the architectural complex in the middle of the nineteenth century. In 1839 Emperor Nicholas I decided to create one more building for the museum of art on a plot of land adjoining the Winter Canal. After its completion in 1852 this became known as the New Hermitage.

While the Hermitage can trace its architectural history back to the first Winter Palaces of Peter the Great, the history of the Hermitage as a museum collection is traditionally held to have begun in 1764. It was in that year that 225 paintings acquired on Catherine II's orders from the Berlin merchant Gotzkowsky arrived on the banks of the Neva. We do not know the exact date when this collection arrived, but the birthday of the Hermitage is celebrated each year on 7 December, the feast day of St Catherine (in honour of its founder).

Following Gotzkowsky's collection, works of great artistic value were acquired for the Empress across the whole of Europe. This process was furthered by the advice and practical assistance of connoisseurs of art (Dmitry

Golitsyn, Alexei Musin-Pushkin, Denis Diderot, Melchior Grimm and many others), as well as the Empress's own undoubted taste. Catherine's Hermitage absorbed the collections of the Prince de Ligne and Count Cobenzl from the Low Countries, Count Brühl from Saxony, Baron Crozat from France, Sir Robert Walpole from England… The museum's stocks grew with extraordinary speed. The first catalogue of the painting collection, published in 1774, already listed some 2,000 works. Apart from paintings, Catherine acquired a host of drawings, engravings, numismatic items, collections of cameos and intaglios, and books, including the libraries of Diderot and Voltaire.

Under Catherine's successors the collections continued to grow. Among the most valuable additions made in the early part of the nineteenth century were the contents of the Malmaison Gallery, formerly the property of Napoleon's first wife, Empress Josephine, acquired by Alexander I; the collection of the Amsterdam banker Coesevelt, and part of that of King William II of the Netherlands, purchased on the orders of Nicholas I.

Nicholas I, who initiated the construction of the New Hermitage, is also connected with the beginning of the tragic practice of mass sales from the Hermitage collections. The Emperor identified a group of paintings that, in his personal opinion, were of little artistic worth and more than a thousand of them were sold at auction. The Hermitage was divested of many of its treasures and subsequently managed to recover only a handful (for example, Chardin's celebrated *Still Life with the Attributes of the Arts*).

Outstanding among the acquisitions of the second half of the nineteenth century and the beginning of the twentieth are two works by Leonardo da Vinci (the *Litta Madonna* was bought in 1865, the *Benois Madonna* in 1914), Basilewsky's collection of mediaeval art, and Semenov-Tian-Shansky's collection of Dutch and Flemish painting.

The First World War and the revolution of 1917 sealed the fate of the main imperial residence. In the summer of 1917 the Winter Palace became the setting for meetings of the Provisional Government. The storming of the palace in October and the overthrow of the Provisional Government opened a new chapter in the history of the former home of the Russian Tsars. A decree of the Military Revolutionary Committee issued on 30 October (Old Style) 1917 declared the Winter Palace to be "a state museum on a par with the Hermitage" and its halls began to be gradually taken over to house the displays of newly-created departments of the Hermitage.

The Hermitage's existence in the post-revolutionary years was full of tragic occurrences. Only towards the end of 1920 did the museum manage to recover its main collections which had been evacuated to Moscow following the outbreak of the First World War and which the Soviet government, having itself moved to Moscow in 1918, considered might be left permanently in the new-old capital. In the event only part of the collection of Old Masters was transferred from the Hermitage to Moscow, for permanent keeping in the Pushkin Museum of Fine Arts. In exchange the Hermitage received from Moscow a share of the works from the collections of Sergei Shchukin and Ivan Morozov. In the 1920s the practice of forming and expanding numerous museums across the USSR by drawing on the stocks of the Hermitage became established and as a consequence many thousands of works went elsewhere. The same period also saw the beginning of the sale of masterpieces from the Hermitage painting collection and works of applied art to buyers abroad. These sales did not, of course, solve the state's financial problems, but they inflicted irreparable damage on the museum. The Hermitage managed to stop the trade in its paintings only in 1934. A reminder of these tragic losses was the opportunity to see Jan van Eyck's *Annunciation*, one of many works sold abroad by the Soviet government, that was kindly returned for a temporary exhibition in 1997 by the National Gallery, Washington.

Severe trials awaited the Hermitage during the Second World War. Before the besieging enemy completely encircled Leningrad, the staff managed to load two trains, sending a considerable part of the museum's collections to the Urals for safekeeping in the Sverdlovsk Picture Gallery. Many items, however, spent all 900 days of the siege in the cellars and ground floor of the museum. Although wounded by bombs and shells, the Hermitage stood firm. In October 1945 the Hermitage collections returned from evacuation and soon the museum reopened its doors to visitors. The restoration of the war-damaged buildings and interiors would take many years, however.

At the same time as the museum was suffering losses in the post-revolutionary years, new directions in research and exhibition activity were being developed within its walls, and new collections being formed. Today the Hermitage is a leading centre of scholarly activity with staff members researching into many aspects of world culture and art. The museum has several research departments, material from whose stocks is included in the permanent display. These are the Departments of the Archaeology of Eastern Europe and Siberia, of the Ancient World, of Western European Art, of the Culture and Art of the Peoples of the East, of the History of Russian Culture, and of Numismatics, as well as the Arsenal, the Menshikov Palace, and the Research Library.

A particular concern for the Hermitage nowadays is to preserve all the wealth of the artistic legacy that it possesses. Specialists of the museum's Department of Scholarly Restoration and Conservation, the staff of the Special Scholarly Restoration Workshops restore thousands of objects of culture and art each year, as well as the priceless Hermitage interiors.

The museum is still constantly expanding its collections. A large share of the acquisitions comes from the Hermitage's archaeological expeditions. Particularly significant collections of archaeological artefacts came into the museum before the late 1980s. The acquisition of new paintings, works of graphic, decorative and applied art, and numismatic items is managed by the Expert Purchasing Commission. A large and particularly important group of new acquisitions comprises the generous gifts of the artists themselves and donations from collectors.

One of the highest priorities in the Hermitage's activities is given to exhibition work. Each year at least twenty temporary exhibitions are held in the museum halls. The tradition of arranging large thematic exhibitions in cities around Russia has been revived. The Hermitage is actively engaged in the exchange of temporary exhibitions with museums abroad. Thanks to this process, in recent years visitors to the Hermitage have been able to acquaint themselves with outstanding works of world art from collections in Western Europe, the United States and Japan.

Recently the International Club of Friends of the Hermitage has been created. National Friends of the Hermitage societies are active in the Netherlands and the United States. Their aims are to strengthen ties with the museum and to support its efforts to preserve the works of culture and art contained within its walls, as well as the whole architectural complex of the museum.

The Hermitage today is not frozen in its evolution; on the contrary, it is an example of a progressively developing museum. The Menshikov Palace on Vasilyevsky Island, which opened its doors to visitors in 1981, has been accorded the status of a branch of the Hermitage. In recent years the museum has been given the "Spare House" — the next building after the Hermitage Theatre on Palace Embankment (the museum's restoration laboratories are beginning to move into it), and also the building once occupied by the Ministries of Foreign Affairs and Finance, where after a thorough reconstruction it is planned to create a Museum of Decorative Art and a computer education centre for all the city's schoolchildren. The annexation of the General Staff building and the organisation of a new entry point for visitors through the Main Gate of the Winter Palace from Palace Square are steps in the collaboration between the Hermitage, the municipal administration and the command of the St Petersburg military district with the aim of developing the entire Palace Square area as a museum-and-ceremonial complex. On 27 May 1998 (the anniversary of the city's foundation) the colourful ceremony of changing the guard at the Winter Palace was reinstated.

At present work is being completed on the Hermitage's new Restoration and Storage Centre in the Staraya Derevnya district. After it opens, the public will have access to many of the museum's stocks. Excursions will take visitors through the rooms where carriages and furniture, easel and monumental paintings are stored. The creation of such a significant cultural institution in the northern districts of St Petersburg will enable the museum to expand the scale of its activities in the field of public education.

In view of the national and international importance of the Hermitage the museum has been included in the list of especially valuable objects of the cultural inheritance of the peoples of the Russian Federation, and in June 1996 Boris Yeltsin took the Hermitage under the particular patronage of the President of the Russian Federation.

And so, on the threshold of the twenty-first century, while preserving the best traditions of one of Russia's oldest museums and remaining a treasure-house of culture and art, the Hermitage looks confidently into the future.

Vladimir Matveyev,
Deputy Director of the State
Hermitage with responsibility
for exhibitions and development

THE WINTER PALACE

    The collections of works of art, gathered together and displayed in
the museum known as the Hermitage, are rightly famous around the world.
The buildings occupied by the museum today — the Winter Palace, Small,
Large and New Hermitages — form one of the finest architectural ensembles
in the central part of St Petersburg, an ensemble that was a century and
a half in the making. Here in the Hermitage complex history presents itself in
all its many aspects; the various facets of the buildings' existence merging
together. Visitors find themselves at one and the same time in the exhibition
halls of one of the greatest museums on the planet, in a special world of
architectural settings designed by some remarkable figures, and in a unique
historical monument — the former residence of the Russian monarchs.

The heart of the Hermitage complex is the Winter Palace, constructed between 1754 and 1762 to the plans of Bartolommeo Francesco Rastrelli (1700–71). The tremendous scale of the building is explained by its intended purpose — to serve as the main residence for the ruler of the Russian Empire. The first Winter Palace appeared in St Petersburg back in the reign of Peter the Great. The choice of the new capital's founder of a site on the bank of the Neva was respected by his successors, successive palaces only shifting closer to the Admiralty. In 1754 Peter's daughter Elizabeth decided on the construction of a new imperial residence. When she died late in 1761, however, the new palace was still not complete and she never lived there. Peter III, who succeeded her, gave orders for the main state rooms and living apartments to be decorated by Easter 1762. The work was carried out and in April the new Tsar and his wife Catherine (the future Catherine II, the Great) moved into the new building. The palace was magnificent. The colours chosen for the façades gave it an exceptional elegance. The walls were painted with "sandy paint with the subtlest shade of yellow, and the ornaments with white lime." The interior decoration was staggering for its richness and variety. The façades of the Winter Palace have generally retained their original appearance (if we disregard the replacement of the sculpture on the parapet in the late nineteenth century and the colour scheme that has changed several times), but the interiors have been repeatedly reworked. Each successive generation of the imperial family adapted the living apartments to its own needs.

Today's Winter Palace preserves the memory of various eras: the creations of Rastrelli's strikingly whimsical architectural fantasy; the state rooms that remind us of official ceremonies; the living apartments decorated in the second half of the nineteenth century drawing on an immense range of architectural prototypes.

The Main Staircase was designed by Rastrelli and when Vasily Stasov restored

the interior after the fire of 1837 he adhered to his predecessor's magnificent
concept. The theatrical effect here stirs the imagination: the low first flight of
the staircase is in shadow and contrasts with the main section where space seems
to open out, reflected in mirrors and bursting out into the infinity of the illusory
painting on the vault. The painted canvas attached to the ceiling in 1839 is by
the eighteenth-century Italian artist Gasparo Diziani and originally adorned
one of the halls of Rastrelli's Winter Palace. This composition, depicting Mount
Olympus, together with the sculptural allegories of Loyalty, Fairness, Majesty,
Wisdom, Justice and Abundance placed in niches pointed to the special function
of the palace as the dwelling place of earthly gods, the home of the virtues.
The staircase gives access to two suites of state rooms, one along the Neva,
the other, main suite, leading to St George's Hall and the Great Church. Walking
through this main suite we follow the course taken by ceremonial processions
from the mid-nineteenth to early twentieth centuries.

The Peter the Great Hall or Small Throne Room is dedicated to the memory
of the founder of the Russian Empire. The hall was created in 1833, to the design
of Auguste de Montferrand (1786–1858), and restored practically without changes
by Stasov after the fire. The dominant feature of the room is the allegorical painting
Peter the Great and Minerva by Jacopo Amiconi. Monograms of Peter the Great,
crowns and double-headed eagles — symbols of imperial power — are prominent
in the decoration of the hall. Paintings depicting the Battles of Poltava and Lesnaya,
two key moments in the Northern War, earned the hall the epithet "palladium
of Russian greatness and glory" (Clausen). Each successive room in this suite
represents one more link in a complex chain of symbolism glorifying Mother Russia.

The Armorial Hall, created by Stasov, was a reminder of the structure
of the state. Originally sculpted figures of Russian warriors stood here holding

The State (Jordan, or Ambassadors') Staircase

spears on the shafts of which were the coats-of-arms of the Russian provinces. Gilded shields bearing the same devices can still be seen on the bronze chandeliers.

The Gallery of 1812 — the most famous of the memorial rooms in the palace — was constructed to a design by Carlo Rossi (1775/77–1849) and ceremonially opened on 25 December 1826, the anniversary of Napoleon's army being driven from Russian soil. The 332 portraits installed here are of those who held the rank of general during the war or were promoted to that rank when it ended. Thirteen places were left empty for dead heroes and others whose likenesses could not be found. Alexander I commissioned the portraits from the George Dawe. The Russian Emperor met the fashionable English portrait-painter in the German city of Aachen where the first congress of the Holy Alliance (countries involved in the defeat of Napoleon) took place in the autumn of 1818. When he came to St Petersburg, besides his official work for the Gallery of 1812, Dawe was literally deluged with commissions from members of the capital's high society and as a result his stay in Russia lasted from 1819 to 1829. All the portraits were saved from the fire in 1837 and later returned to their places. Dawe's depiction of Alexander I was replaced by a grander equestrian portrait of the Emperor painted by Franz Krüger. The gallery formed a fitting prelude to entering the "heart" of the Winter Palace — St George's Hall.

St George's Hall or the Large Throne Room is where the symphony of magnificent architectural settings reached its climax. The new throne room was

The Silver Throne of Empress Anna Ioannovna. By Nicholas Clausen. 1731

The Hall of Peter the Great

Plat de ménage. 1727
France. Claude Ballin
Silver

The *plat de ménage* was
a fashionable kind of table
decoration in the eighteenth
century consisting of a tray
base with a fruit bowl, flower
vase, candle holders,
and vessels for spices
and condiments attached.
The Hermitage's collection
of Western European silver
is considered one of the best
in the world. The items
produced by French
eighteenth-century
craftsmen are noted for
particularly exquisite forms
and virtuoso detail work.
Luxury items — gala dinner
services, wine vessels and
coolers, candelabra, toilet
and writing sets, fans
and toys — can be seen
in the showcases of
the Armorial Hall.

created for Catherine II in 1787–95 by Giacomo Quarenghi (1744–1817) in a
special extension built onto the palace within the great courtyard. The decoration
of the throne room in Rastrelli's Winter Palace was never fully completed as
Catherine found the opulent whimsy of the Baroque old-fashioned and out of tune
with the rational ideals of the Age of Enlightenment. The new throne room was
decorated in strict Classical manner. The immense hall with two tiers of windows
astonished contemporaries, but Quarenghi's masterpiece perished in the fire of
1837. Emperor Nicholas I gave orders to "try to make St George's Hall … entirely
of white marble" and consequently Stasov did not restore the facing of the walls
and columns in various different shades of marble. The white Carrara marble

The Gallery of 1812

that endows the throne room with such an air of solemn grandeur was brought specially from Italy.

The ceiling was adorned with gilded ornamentation, the pattern of which is repeated in a parquet floor made of sixteen kinds of colourful wood. Due to the amount of work involved in the marble facing, Stasov completed St George's Hall later than the other restored rooms and it was consecrated in 1841. The hall played its part in all the official history of Russia's ruling house. The "great

All the portraits in the Gallery of 1812 were painted in the studio of George Dawe, an English artist who was invited to Russia by Alexander I specially to do this one job.

George Dawe
*Portrait of Field Marshal
Kutuzov. 1829*

George Dawe
*Portrait of the Grenadier
Ilya Yamnik. 1828*

26

Гренадеръ Илья Ямникъ

St George's Hall

*The throne
in St George's Hall*

entrees" of the imperial family — formal processions from the private apartments through the state rooms of the Neva and Main Suites — ended either in the Large Throne Room or in the Great Church.

The Great Church, elevated to the status of a cathedral in 1807, was created by Rastrelli at the time of the palace's construction and consecrated to the Resurrection in 1762. In 1763, when an icon of the Vernicle (a traditional, supposedly miraculous image of Christ) was installed here, it was reconsecrated as the Church of the Vernicle. After the great fire Stasov was instructed to restore the church to its former appearance. The architect strove to recreate the Baroque elements and follow Rastrelli's original concept. He gave the church back its dome that had been covered over long before the fire. A large part of the decoration here was produced in papier-mâché that provided a useful alternative to time-consuming wood-carving in view of the brief period allotted to the restoration of the Winter Palace. The idea of using this material first occurred to Stasov in 1820 when he was restoring the palace church at Tsarskoye Selo. The splendid iconostasis by the master carver Cretan was disassembled in the 1940s.

A small passageway connects the state rooms to the living area of the Winter

The dome
of the Great Church

The bell-tower
of the Great Church

The interior
of the Great Church

Palace. These, once the private dwelling place of all the Russian rulers and their families, from Catherine II to Nicholas II, the quarters for ladies- and gentlemen-in-waiting, and ancillary rooms, spread over three storeys of the palace now house some of the exhibits that make the Hermitage such a rich museum. The Departments of Primitive Culture, Russian Culture and the East were formed in Soviet times. Thanks to them, the Hermitage, which since the beginning of the nineteenth century had been famous as one of the finest collections of Western European painting, earned the right to be regarded as one of the major repositories of the world's cultural artefacts. The treasures of Scythian burial-mounds and Sassanid silver from Iran, Persian carpets and Chinese porcelain, the sculpture of Ancient Egypt and Byzantine icons, coins, jewellery, weapons,

Etienne Maurice Falconet
Cupid Wagging His Finger
1757

Falconet (1716–91) was a
celebrated French sculptor
of the Rococo era. In 1767
he came to Russia at
the invitation of Catherine II
to work on the "Bronze
Horseman" monument
to Peter the Great. All the
works by Falconet now in
the Hermitage were created
before he left France. This
Cupid was one of the most
popular statues of
the eighteenth century,
known from a large number
of replicas' The elegant
figure of the little god
of love, full of easy grace,
was commissioned by
the sculptor's patroness,
the Marquise de Pompadour
to decorate a "temple
of love" in the garden.

In the south wing of
the palace in 1838–39
Alexander Briullov created
a suite of five state rooms in
which a collection of battle
paintings inspired by events
in Russian eighteenth- and
nineteenth-century martial
history. Originally this
area was living quarters,
including, alongside
the Great Church,
the apartments of Catherine
the Great. In the south-east,
in the attics some exquisitely
decorated rooms were
created that from the 1780s
were used to display oriental
curios and objects of applied
art. It was these "Chinese"
attics that Catherine II
called her "hermitage".

ivory, metal and wooden articles, stones worked by Russian craftsmen and
the works of celebrated artists of Peter the Great's time. The most precious part
of the Hermitage's stocks, first and foremost the Western European painting, came
into the museum through the collecting activities of the Russian rulers.

In 1764 Catherine the Great acquired a large collection of paintings by Western
European artists from the Prussian merchant Johann Ernst Gotzkowsky and
so laid the foundation for the Hermitage's picture gallery. Within a short time
the Russian Empress's collection could justly lay claim to one of the first places
in the world for both the quantity and the quality of the works that it included.

The "Northern Minerva", as Catherine was known in Europe, sought
as quickly as possible to make her holdings the equal of the celebrated royal
collections of Vienna and Paris, thus elevating the prestige of the Russian court
and her own reputation as an enlightened monarch. As Catherine herself
admitted, she understood nothing about painting and relied entirely for
the selection of works on intermediaries who included some of the century's
most brilliant minds — the philosopher Denis Diderot, the man of letters
Melchior Grimm, and the diplomat Dmitry Golitsyn.

During Catherine's reign the Hermitage came into possession of many
outstanding paintings, notably first-rate products of the Dutch and Flemish
schools, with the oeuvres of Rembrandt, Rubens and Van Dyck particularly
well represented. Through the efforts of Diderot superb examples of French
seventeenth- and eighteenth-century painting found their way to St Petersburg.
Towards the end of the century works by Italian Renaissance artists were acquired,
while the Netherlandish, German, Spanish and English schools were represented
by outstanding individual pieces.

In the Empress's day all these treasures hung in the halls of the Winter Palace,
and also in the buildings of the Small and Large (Old) Hermitages that Catherine
had built specifically for them. There, apart from the owner herself, they could
be seen only by members of the court, and foreign travellers, artists and students
of the Academy of Arts who were granted special permission. By the middle
of the nineteenth century the collection of Western European painting had for
the most part been formed, but right up to the early twentieth century additions
were being made. Today's Hermitage picture gallery bears little resemblance
to Catherine the Great's "place of solitude".

The former living quarters and service rooms of the Winter Palace are now
given over to collections that cover a period from prehistoric times to the present
century: from artefacts uncovered by archaeological excavations and the works of
Oriental craftsmen to masterpieces of Western European painting and sculpture.

The strikingly rich and varied collection of French art from the fifteenth
to twentieth centuries occupies about fifty rooms in the Winter Palace.

The collection is rightly considered one of the most significant and complete
in the Hermitage's stocks. It occupies some fifty rooms in the museum and
covers practically all styles and trends in French art, presenting leading painters,
sculptors and masters of applied art. No other collection outside of France can
compete with the Hermitage for quantity and quality of splendid products
of the refined Gallic culture. Many of them were acquired at the instigation of
Catherine II who was reckoned a great admirer of French style and French fashion.

The great seventeenth-century artist Nicolas Poussin (1594–1665) — creator
and head of the French Classical school — is represented in the Hermitage by
twelve works. The greater part of Poussin's life was spent in Italy, far from Paris

The Hall of French Rococo Art

and the royal court with its strict rules and demands on an artist. In the atmosphere of falsehood and hypocrisy that prevailed at the court of Louis XIII, where the straightforward, noble-minded artist became the target of lies, envy and hatred from his fellows, particularly Simon Vouet, Poussin would never have attained greatness. Only in Italy, a country he adored, could the painter develop freely, following his own aesthetic tastes and convictions. The study of Classical monuments and Renaissance masterpieces coupled with reflection on the character of perfection and harmony in nature and in art led Poussin to create the theory and practice of Classicism — a balanced, elevated style that celebrated the triumph of human reason.

Landscape with Polyphemus (1649) is a glorious dream of an ancient "Golden Age", of a world in which people, gods and animals live in harmony with the natural setting that is beautiful and eternal. It was probably this very work to which Poussin was referring to when he wrote in a letter: "Paintings that possess perfection should not be viewed in haste, but slowly examined, evaluating, and with understanding…"

At first glance the *Dairymaid's Family* by Louis Le Nain (1593–1648) seems a humble scene of daily life in comparison with Poussin's magnificent creations. The painting, produced in the 1640s, belongs to what is known as the peasant genre, of which Louis Le Nain was reckoned the greatest exponent. Yet Le Nain's

Vouet (1590–1649) was
the first painter to King
Louis XIII, one of the
creators of the official,
elevated style. His majestic
canvases on historical and
allegorical subjects are full
of grand, rather cool
rhetoric and bombast. This
portrait is a grand allegorical
depiction of the Queen, wife
of Louis XIII and mother
of the future Sun-King
Louis XIV, in the guise of
Minerva, the Ancient Roman
goddess of wisdom, with
attributes of power and
wisdom — the helmet,
shield, sceptre and owl.

*Dish. 16th century. France.
Workshop of Bernard Palissy*

Palissy (ca. 1510–89) was one
of the most outstanding
figures in France for
the breadth and depth of
his knowledge, a typical
"Renaissance man".
He studied chemistry
and natural sciences, was a
writer, an artist and a garden
architect. He invented
the clear lead glaze that he
used to create his celebrated
"Palissy ware" — pottery
decorated with reliefs
depictions of frogs, fish,
lizards and snakes.

peasants are full of the same sense of majesty as Poussin's mythological or biblical
characters. The figures of the elderly countrywoman, the old man, boy and girl
gathered around the donkey that is the mainstay of their existence are super-
ficially almost totally inactive; they are frozen against the background of an
immense silvery-blue sky and a distant hilly landscape. Every detail here seems
real and accurate in the extreme, but at the same time this relatively small work
is full of the true artistry and genuine monumental quality characteristic
of the finest examples of French Classicism.

The suite of rooms running alongside the courtyard of the Winter Palace,
parallel to the displays of French sixteenth- and seventeenth-century art, contains
German art of the fifteenth to eighteenth centuries. This collection cannot lay
claim to the fullness or variety of the French. The age of the German Renaissance
is represented here through one of its greatest artists — Lucas Cranach the Elder
(1472–1553). The Hermitage possesses four paintings by Cranach. Particularly

Nicolas Poussin
Landscape with Polyphemus
1649

The Adoration of the Magi
Central part of a triptych
Early 16th century
Limoges, France. Enamel

Painted enamels, produced
primarily for religious
purposes — images of saints,
folding domestic altarpieces
became a speciality of
Limoges before the end
of the Middle Ages.
The technique involved was
highly complicated: copper
plaques were covered with
layer of opaque white
enamel. After firing a design
was outlined on it with black
paint and then painted in
with transparent enamel
colours. The main difficulty
of this process lay in the fact
that the piece had to be fired
10–15 times, as each colour
required a particular
temperature. In the fifteenth
century multicoloured
enamels were with gold paint
and cabochons — large
drops of translucent enamel
placed on pieces of gold
or silver foil in imitation
of precious stones.

noteworthy among them is *Venus and Cupid* (1509), the artist's earliest work on
the subject. It is believed that this painting was the first attempt made in northern
Europe to depict the goddess of love and beauty naked. In Germany at the time
of the Reformation the image of Venus was associated with the sin of lechery, hence
the Latin inscription towards the top of the work that warns: "Reject Cupid's
sensuality with all your might, else Venus will take possession of your blinded soul."

On the whole, however, the modest stock of German painting serves to stress
even more clearly the wealth and range of the French collection, particularly
the eighteenth century. It was at that time that France firmly captured

Louis Le Nain
Dairymaid's Family. 1640s

33

Lucas Cranach the Elder
Female Portrait. 1526

PELLE · CVPIDINEOS · TOTO   CONAMINE · LVXVS
NE · TVA · POSSIDEAT   PECTORA · CECA · VENVS

Lucas Cranach the Ekder. Venus and Cupid. 1509

the European art market and the Rococo style that emerged then became the yardstick of taste, elegance and luxury. Celebrated porcelain services produced by the craftsmen of the Sèvres factory, an immense stock of tapestries, exquisite Rococo furniture, and decorative pieces made of bronze and silver give a special atmosphere to the halls that house the works of the greatest artists of the century, the age when French culture triumphed.

The Hermitage can boast eight paintings by Antoine Watteau, twelve by François Boucher, and several first-rate canvases by Jean-Baptiste Siméon Chardin and Jean-Honoré Fragonard. The sculpture of this period is represented by works from its finest masters — Etienne Maurice Falconet and Jean Antoine Houdon.

Antoine Watteau (1684–1721) was the founding father of a style that determined the character of French art in the eighteenth century — the virtuoso artistry of the Rococo. Yet Watteau's paintings, for all their immediately dazzling mastery, are complex and contradictory like the personality of the artist himself. *A Capricious Woman* (ca. 1718) is considered one of the finest examples what is known as the *fête galante*, a genre invented by Watteau in which the subject revolves around the characters' barely detectable feelings. The painter often left his paintings untitled, stressing the fact that for him the important thing was not a narrative plot, but a particular emotional state expressed by purely painterly means — through rhythm, colour scheme and movement.

The Alexander Hall

In 1834 Alexander Briullov drew up a plan for a hall dedicated to the memory of Alexander I that was realised after the great fire. The architect found a brilliant spatial and constructional solution for the immense hall with two tiers of windows. The original ceiling design with fan vaults supporting shallow domes became the chief feature of the Alexander Hall. The tremendous airiness and the grandeur of the spaces beneath the domes caused contemporaries to speak of the room being " in the Byzantine taste". In the decoration the architect also used elements of another style — the Gothic: bundles of slender columns and the fan vaulting which serve to stress the sense of upward motion in the architectural masses. The hall perpetuated the memory of Alexander I (a portrait of the Emperor by George Dawe was placed on the end wall and above it a bas-relief depicting Alexander in profile "in the guise of the Slavonic deity Rodomysl" — the embodiment of wisdom and courage) and of the "Patriotic War" of 1812 and subsequent foreign campaign by the Russian army. The frieze was adorned by enlarged copies of the medals designed by Fiodor Tolstoi, that tell of those events in an allegorical way, and symbolic figures of Glory. The main element in the moulded decoration are compositions of military accoutrements. In contrast to the Gallery of 1812 which recalled specific heroes of the war against Napoleon, the Alexander Hall reminded people of that highly important event in Russia history through images and allusions. The memorial character of the hall was underlined by four immense battle scenes painted by Gottfried Willewalde.

The French master craftsmen
— cabinet-makers,
woodcarvers, silversmiths
who worked to commissions
from the French kings in this
period were no less famous
in Europe than their artist
and sculptor compatriots.
Apart from the best
collection of silver in
the world, the Hermitage
possesses some splendid
works by the craftsmen of
the Sèvres porcelain factory,
royal Gobelins tapestries and
furniture that are displayed
in the halls of the Winter
Palace. The pride of
the Hermitage furniture
collection are the pieces
by the court cabinet-maker
André Charles Boulle who
worked around the turn
of the eighteenth century.
In France *cabinet* was
the word used for superbly
finished pieces of furniture
with a large number of
drawers for storing money,
valuables, coin and medal
collections. A cupboard
produced in Boulle's
workshop is a magnificent
sight. Its doors are decorated
with marquetry depictions
of bouquets in precious
varieties of wood set into
a tortoiseshell background as
well as inlaid brass and tin.
This extremely rare exhibit
is one of a pair; the other
is in France.

Striking mastery, freedom and immediacy in the treatment of his subject
were demonstrated by Jean-Honoré Fragonard (1732–1806) in *The Stolen Kiss*
(late 1780s). This masterpiece by the darling of the Parisian public — "Frago"
as he was affectionately known to his numerous advisors — came into
the Hermitage in the late nineteenth century from the former collection
of the last King of Poland, Stanislas Poniatowski.

Saying Grace by Jean-Baptiste Siméon Chardin (1699–1779) simply oozes
persuasive verisimilitude and naturalness. Yet even in the real world where
Chardin's humble heroines have their existence, a French artist of the second
half of the eighteenth century managed to find the spirituality, harmony and
poetry so characteristic of the works of his great predecessors — Poussin,
Le Nain and Watteau.

Adjoining the halls of eighteenth-century French art is a relatively small

*Cameo Service. 1778–79
Sèvres porcelain factory,
France*

This service, striking for its
elegant forms and refined
combinations of colour, was
produced at the Sèvres
factory for Catherine II.

In March 1778 the Empress wrote to her constant correspondent Melchior Grimm: "The Sèvres service that I have ordered is intended for the greatest lover of nail-biting, my dear, beloved Prince Potemkin, but in order that the service be as good as possible I am saying that it is for me." The pieces are decorated with depictions of ancient cameos alternating with plant ornament on a background of turquoise with gilding. Garlands of flowers form the Empress's monogram. During the fire of 1837 about 160 items from this service were stolen. Ten years later they turned up at auction in London. The efforts of Russian diplomats succeeded in returning them to the Winter Palace. Today there are 688 pieces in the Hermitage collection.

The Hall of Eighteenth-Century French Art

collection of English art. The paintings and pieces of applied art displayed here nonetheless give an adequate impression of the distinctive qualities of the English school.

English art reached its highest point in the work of two outstanding eighteenth-century painters: Thomas Gainsborough (1727–88) and Joshua Reynolds (1723–92). The first president of the Royal Academy and head of the English school, Sir Joshua was celebrated first and foremost for his paintings. Four works in the Hermitage collection give us an idea of the "historical compositions" to which the artist turned his hand quite rarely. *Cupid Untying the Girdle of Venus* is one of the artist's own replicas on a popular subject of the day, but the figures in the painting are far removed from the Classical ideal. Venus is an entirely real, flesh-and-blood English beauty, with a rosy complexion and red hair looking out coquettishly at the viewer in feigned bewilderment at the dangerous game being played by the naughty urchin Cupid.

Jean-Honoré Fragonard
The Stolen Kiss. Late 1780s

Antoine Watteau
A Capricious Woman
Ca. 1718

Gainsborough's *Portrait of a Lady in Blue* is marked by the poetic spiritual quality that was the hallmark of this subtle, refined artist. The depiction of the woman on the canvas resembles some exquisite flower created in a harmony of silver, grey and blue tones.

The remarkable collection of French nineteenth- and early-twentieth-century painting housed in third-floor rooms reflects all the complex, at times dramatic struggle between different tendencies, the changes of styles and leaders that characterized the art of this period. The first tendency, which established itself towards the end of the eighteenth century, on the eve of the French Revolution was Neo-Classicism, represented here by the works of pupils and followers of the school's

Jean-Baptiste Siméon Chardin. Saying Grace. 1744

39

Joshua Reynolds
Cupid Untying the Girdle
of Venus. 1788

The Green Frog Service
1773–74. Wedgwood factory,
England

Catherine II commissioned
this service for a "wayside
palace" (later called
the Chesme Palace) located
outside St Petersburg on the
road to Moscow. The locality
was known in the Finnish
of the local peasantry as
Kekerekeksinen — "the frog
marsh". Hence the emblem
on the service: a green
frog on a heraldic shield.
The service was intended
for 50 diners and included
dinner (680 pieces decorated
with garlands of oak-leaves)
and desert (264 pieces
decorated with ivy leaves)
sections. Each item was
individually painted with
a different, true-to-life
view of a place in England.
While working on the service
Josiah Wedgwood (1730–95)
perfected the traditional
English creamware pottery,
calling his variety "Queen's
Ware" in honour of his
patroness Queen Charlotte.

head, Jacques-Louis David (1748–1825). We can judge the first, revolutionary, stage
of the new Classicism from the painting *Napoleon on the Bridge at Arcola* created
by one of David's most loyal pupils, Jean Antoine Gros (1771–1835). Artists of this
tendency usually painted subjects from the Ancient World, Roman history being
especially popular, and sought out examples of fidelity to great ideas. For them
Napoleon was practically the only contemporary whose martial deeds in the name
of his country could stand alongside those of ancient heroes.

The work by David himself to be found in the Hermitage, *Sappho and Phaon*,
belongs to the late stage of Classicism, when the "ancient cries of the revolution"

Thomas Gainsborough
Portrait of a Lady in Blue
Late 1770s

Tub wine-cooler. 1720s
England. By Paul
de Lamerie. Silver

The Hermitage has one
of the best collections of
English silver. The majority
of noted silversmiths active
in England in the first-half of
the eighteenth century were
Huguenots of French origin.
The style of de Lamerie
(1688–1751) was marked by
elegance and a truly Gallic
lightness. With good reason
his works became a yardstick
of refinement and virtuoso
skill. This tub-shaped wine-
cooler is not only a splendid
decorative work, but also,
when filled with ice and
bottles, served a very
practical purpose.

41

*Jean Antoine Gros
Napoleon on the Bridge
at Arcola. 1796*

The subject of this painting
is founded on a real event.
The Battle of Arcola
(15–17 November 1796)
between the French and
the Austrians ended in
a French victory, due in
great part to the heroism
of the young General
Napoleon Bonaparte.

had died down. David became first painter to Napoleon, the new Emperor
of France. Everything in the painting would seem to follow the traditions of Neo-
Classicism — from the ideally beautiful images of the Ancient Greek poetess
and her lover to the details of furniture and clothing that David sketched from

*Edgar Delacroix
Lion Hunt in Morocco. 1854*

Jacques-Louis David
Sappho and Phaon. 1809

authentic works of ancient art. But the Ancient World serves here to express
tender feelings, rather than extol civic virtues.

The Classical system had a great many adherents in France, but even the most
convinced sometimes found themselves constricted by its rigid framework.
In the 1820s it collapsed, giving way, not without a fight, to Romanticism.
The greatest of the French Romanticists, Eugène Delacroix (1798–1863),
is represented in the Hermitage by two works dating from the 1850s, when
Romanticism had long since established its right to exist, yet they still carry
the dynamism and energy of that heroic age.

Realism, which succeeded Romanticism, began with the landscapes of
the Barbizon school. It was the members of that school, Théodore Rousseau, Jules
Dupré, Charles Daubigny, the celebrated master of the landscape Camille Corot,
and also the great Realists of the middle of the century, François Millet, Gustave
Courbet and Honoré Daumier, who became the true teachers of a new generation
of French painters known as the Impressionists. The Hermitage's stock of works
representing the main trends of the second half of the nineteenth and early
twentieth centuries — Impressionism, Post-Impressionism, Fauvism, Cubism —
is justly considered one of the finest in the world. Claude Monet and his kindred
spirits, Auguste Renoir, Edgar Degas, Camille Pissarro and Alfred Sisley, struggled
against the hidebound traditions of Classical art, striving to regenerate painting by
getting closer to nature — a lighter palette, directly conveying impressions from
everyday life, yet they did not spurn the great legacy of the artists of the past.
The works of Le Nain, Poussin, Watteau, Chardin and Fragonard remained for

Auguste Renoir
Portrait of the Actress
Jeanne Samary. 1878

them great examples for study, the true school by which to master painting.
The participants of the first Impressionist exhibition in 1874 also included Paul
Cézanne (1839–1906), but in contrast to his fellows there, he did not strive only
to convey impressions of the real world. He dreamed of turning Impressionism
into a kind of art that would be "eternal, solid, like the art of the museums".

Like the Impressionists, Cézanne worked outdoors, but the objects in his still
lifes are not dissolved by the air, turning into patches of colour, but have the same

density and material quality as in the works of the Old Masters; only he does not achieve it by gradations of light and shade, but by the alternation of warm and cold colours.

The painting of the tormented Dutch-born Vincent van Gogh (1853–90) was also to a large extent founded on the achievements, but colour in his paintings is more active than it is in life. For him the colour scheme was above all an expression of the feelings and emotions that possessed him while he worked. In essence Van Gogh used impressions from life as a means to express his own spiritual states.

Vincent van Gogh
Lilac Bush. 1889

Vincent van Gogh
Cottages. 1890

The four Hermitage paintings by Van Gogh were painted in the last, most dramatic
period of the artist's life. At Arles in 1888 he painted *Memories of the Garden
at Etten* (1888) and *The Arena in Arles* (1888). In the following year he produced
The Lilac Bush in the garden of the hospital at Saint-Rémy. *Cottages*, created
in Auvers-sur-Oise, dates from 1890, the year of his tragic death.

The third figure who stands alongside Cézanne and Van Gogh at the sources of
twentieth-century art is Paul Gauguin (1848–1903). The three, for all their apparent
complete disparity of tastes, passions, origins and education, nonetheless had much
in common: as lone rebels they each started from Impressionism and devised their

Paul Gauguin
Woman Holding a Fruit. 1893

Auguste Rodin. Bust of Vera
Yeliseyeva. 1906. Marble

The work of Auguste Rodin
(1840–1917) opened a new
page in the evolution of
Western European sculpture
in the late nineteenth and
early twentieth centuries.
The outstanding French
sculptor is represented in
the Hermitage by pieces from
various stages in his career.
The collection opens with
a plaster cast that was used
for the casting in metal of
the celebrated statue *The Age
of Brass (L'Age d'Airain)* that
marked the start of Rodin's
complex, contradictory path
towards the regeneration
of plastic form. A number
of later works are connected
with the concept to which the
sculptor devoted his life but
which was destined never to
be fully realised — the *Gates
of Hell*, a cycle of sculptures
and reliefs intended to decorate the entrance to the
Museum of Decorative Arts
in Paris. The sketches became
works of art in their own
right. The marble group
Eternal Spring, known from
numerous copies, is probably
the most popular example
of such a transformation.
The bust of Vera Yeliseyeva
was created in Rodin's studio
in 1906, at a time when
the style of the once-scorned
sculptor had become publicly
accepted as a stan-dard for
contemporary art. The bust
was carved in marble not
by Rodin himself but by his
pupil, the future celebrated
sculptor Charles Despiau.

own method. As a result they are customarily known as the Post-Impressionists.

The Hermitage collection includes fifteen works by Gauguin, dating from
the period he spent on Tahiti. Gauguin imagined life on the remote Pacific island
to be something like paradise, a Golden Age in which the artist hoped to recover
something European civilization had lost — the sense of harmony and balance
necessary to produce perfect works of art. Gauguin treated the Tahitian
environment and the inhabitants of that beautiful country in a highly stylized
manner, although his painting is based on real-life impressions. His painterly
system was close to the mediaeval technique of cloisonné enamel or stained glass,
in which coloured surfaces destroy shadows, creating a refined play of painterly
patches. Gauguin's paintings are often filled with an eccentric mixture of

Paul Gauguin
Sunflowers. 1901

Christian, mythological, Oriental and pagan symbols, rhythmically intertwined with specific images from life. The symbolism in Gauguin's works is intriguingly mysterious and full of half-hints.

Gauguin's influence can be clearly felt in the work of the group of artists calling themselves Nabis (Hebrew for *prophets*) who came together at the end of the 1880s. The name of the group was intended to stress the particular spirituality and intellectual elitism of its members. Drawing on religion, philosophy and the mystical teachings of the East, the Nabi artists wanted

Paul Signac
The Harbour at Marseilles
1906

In conjunction with Georges Seurat, Paul Signac (1863–1935) developed in the late 1880s a new manner of working that became known variously as Neo-Impressionism, Divisionism or Pointillism. This new Impressionism took the form of painting with small separate (hence Divisionism) dabs of colour and was founded on precise scientific knowledge of physical principles relating to the blending of shades of colour. The Neo-Impressionists contrasted their method to the spontaneity of the Impressionist glimpse of the world.

*Henri Rousseau. The Chopin
Monument in the Jardin
du Luxembourg. 1909*

Henri Rousseau (1844–
1910), who worked in
the Paris customs office
(hence his nickname
"Douanier Rousseau"),
was a "Sunday painter",
an amateur. But his naive,
sincere art caught the
attention of professional
artists, above all Renoir,
Degas, Gauguin and Picasso,
and eventually went down
in the history of French art
as a separate, original
phenomenon. The world
of Rousseau's images is
divorced from reality,
although often inspired
by specific events or places.
The artist created his own
world, frozen, full of mystery
and the fantastic play
of whimsical forms.

*Henri Rousseau. The Chopin
Monument in the Jardin
du Luxembourg. 1909*

*Vase in the form of a peach-
tree trunk with fruit. 18th
century. China. Chalcedony*

Located in the second-floor
rooms of the Winter Palace,
alongside the collection of
later French art, is a display
of Chinese art spanning
a period from the fourteenth
century B.C. to the twentieth
century. The core of the
collection is superb examples
of Chinese applied art —
porcelain and articles made
from semiprecious stone
and enamel.

*Pierre Bonnard
Evening in Paris. 1911*

to make contemporary art elevated and eternal.

Maurice Denis (1870–1943) began with admiration of Gauguin, whom
he considered a modern-day prophet, gradually shifted towards Poussin,
Fra Angelico and Raphael. The attempt to create "sacred art" made Denis
tackle monumental canvases on Old and New Testament subjects. His paintings

Maurice Denis
The Sacred Grove. 1897

are dense with symbolism, frequently requiring a certain erudition from
the viewer in order to appreciate the meaning contained within them.

Pierre Bonnard (1864–1947) was less inclined than others in the group
to abstract speculative theories. In his work he followed the Impressionists, but,
having gone through the school of Gauguin and Cézanne, he painted from life
depicting Parisian streets and Mediterranean landscapes. Bonnard did not strive
only to convey real-life impressions. He preserved the conventional character
of the canvas, stressing that colour combinations and the painter's brushstrokes
had a value in themselves.

Pablo Picasso (1881–1973) and Henri Matisse (1869–1954) — two of
the greatest artists of the twentieth century —are represented in the Hermitage
by some of the finest examples of their work. It was their art that particularly
attracted the Russian industrialist Sergei Shchukin, who before the First World
War bought what seemed their boldest works, puzzling his fellow collectors. It is to
Shchukin's collection that we owe all the thirty-plus Picassos in the Hermitage.

Figurine of a lion
18th century. China
Porcelain, painted enamel

Pablo Picasso
Woman with a Fan. 1908

They date from the three early period of his career — Blue, Pink and Cubist.

The Absinthe Drinker (1901) was painted by the twenty-year-old Picasso soon after he moved from Spain to Paris. The motif, very popular with French artists, here acquires a dramatic, acutely psychological tone uncharacteristic of

Pablo Picasso
The Visit (Sisters). 1902

contemporary French painting. These qualities became even stronger in the works of the Blue Period, so called because of Picasso's predilection for the colour dark blue that expresses feelings of loneliness, melancholy, sadness and suffering shared.

A tragic sense of hopelessness emanates powerfully from *The Visit* (*Sisters*) (1902), one of the key works of the Blue Period.

The story of this canvas gives us an idea of how a real-life impression might inspire Picasso to a composition that can stand comparison with the art of the Old Masters, particularly the Spaniards Ribera, Zurbarán and Morales. Originally Picasso intended to paint the meeting between two sisters, a nun and a prostitute, by the walls of the Saint-Lazare prison hospital. Gradually, however, as he worked on the idea, the indications of time and place grew increasingly abstract. Finally Picasso left on the canvas only two, almost identical female figures dressed in dark blue, rendered ageless, located in a timeless, cold, blue-green space. The tragedy of human loneliness, expressed with extreme drama here, was to be one of the chief themes in Picasso's output.

In 1906 Picasso moved on to Cubism. Now he was creating his own world based on the laws of geometry and logic. On the one hand Cubism is founded of Cézanne's celebrated formula: "everything in nature can be pictured in the form of a sphere, a cylinder and a cone." On the other on the geometrical simplicity and inner freedom of Black African sculpture.

Henri Matisse
The Painter's Family. 1911

In *Woman with a Fan* (1908) all the details of the face and body are reduced
to simplified forms, combinations of curved and straight-edged volumes.
Yet this geometrical image, seemingly hewn from hard rock does not lose its
emotional impact — the pose, gesture and inclined head express a sense
of tiredness and concentration.

Henri Matisse founded his work on the leading role of colour; asserting with
each picture the idea that "an artist should possess the gift of colour, like a singer
his voice." Like Picasso, he became the creator of a new tendency — Fauvism
(from *fauves*, meaning "wild beasts"). In 1905 a group of young artists headed
by Matisse caused the official critics to literally explode with disapproval at
the Salon d'Automne when they came across their bright, unfettered paintings
screaming with tense combinations of paints. Covering his canvas with blue, red
and green, bringing them together in jarring chords, Matisse sort after the ultimate
concentration of feelings that could be expressed through a patch of colour.

The Red Room (1908) might be called Matisse's programmatic work, one in
which all his principles are most precisely expressed. The red colour here is like
a musical instrument in an orchestra playing solo. The original composition
looked different, though, and was called *Harmony in Blue* with a dominant role
being taken by the pale blue drapery.

The artist has turned all the elements of the picture — the still life on the table, the figure of the woman, the table and chairs, and the landscape outside the window — into flat patches of colour, rhythmically echoing the ornament of the decorative fabric that organizes space on the canvas.

In *The Painter's Family* (1911) Matisse attempted a new interpretation of a traditional genre. Reflecting on the art of portraiture, he said that portraitists had been overtaken by photographers and therefore nothing remained for artists to do but to enhance colour and design in their depictions. When painting his own wife and children in the interior of a living room, Matisse first and foremost united in a single harmonious whole the ornament of the brightly coloured carpet, the design of the wallpaper and the geometric pattern of the chessboard using the large pure patches of colour — the red of the boys' shirts and the black of his daughter's dress.

The Dutchman Kees van Dongen (1877–1968) became a fashionable portrait-painter, revealing the extravagant, sinful life of Paris's artistic bohemians to the wider public. His heroines are *femmes fatales*, dangerous, aggressive, driven by determination to attract, conquer and seduce.

The landscapes of Maurice Vlaminck (1876–1958) are gaunt and dramatic. Although he went through the "trial by colour" of Fauvism, this artist nevertheless had a greater sense of an inner affinity with Van Gogh and Cézanne. His palette is expressive and full of tension; his linear rhythms impulsive and staccato.

André Derain (1880–1954) shared a studio with Vlaminck in the Parisian suburb Chatou during the Fauve period. At first passionately devoted to the same ideas as Matisse, he soon took a rapid turn in the direction of Cubism. Landscape *The Grove* Derain's palette has become drab, twilit, composed of dull grey, brownish and greenish combinations in which the trees no longer look like bright flat patches.

The flowering of French art in the nineteenth and early twentieth centuries

Carpet (detail)
5th century B.C.
Pazyryk Burial-Mound

The halls on the ground floor of the Winter Palace contain extremely precious exhibits belonging to the Department of Primitive Culture. First and foremost they are artefacts from burials made by nomadic tribes in the Altai, Siberia and the south of Russia in the fifth and fourth centuries B.C. In the Pazyryk Valley in the Altai between 1927 and 1949 some priceless items were discovered that had been created more than 2,500 years ago and splendidly preserved by the unusual conditions prevailing in the burial mounds. Frozen soil formed beneath the artificial mound of stones. Water permeated into it, but the sun never reached it, creating conditions similar to permafrost. Because of this, the graves of tribal chieftains were found to contain not only stone artefacts, but wooden items, the mummies of human beings and the bodies of horses , fabrics, clothing and provisions — in a word, everything that is usually lost with time. The felt carpet, with an area of 30 square metres (320 square feet), was originally on the wall of the log-built burial-chamber.

Henri Matisse
The Red Room. 1908

Maurice de Vlaminck
View of the Seine. 1905–06

Kees van Dongen
Red Dancer. Ca. 1907

seems all the more outstanding when compared to the painting produced in neighbouring countries in the same period. The second-floor rooms overlooking the courtyard contain a relatively small display of art from German, Italy and other European states. Naturally it is difficult to compare collections that are tremendously different in quantity and quality, but despite their disparateness and randomness, these works by artists of other schools do make it possible to trace certain national peculiarities.

The collection of nineteenth- and early-twentieth-century German painting should be particularly singled out. The Hermitage possesses one of the world's finest sets of paintings by Caspar David Friedrich (1774–1840), one of the foremost representatives of German Romanticism. Almost all of the nine works came to Russia during Friedrich's own lifetime, offered by Friedrich first to Emperor Nicholas I and then to the poet Vasily Zhukovsky who was tutor to Nicholas's heir. *On a Sailing-Ship* (1818–19) is more poetic dream than reality. The man and woman seated in the prow have their backs to the viewer and are gazing intently at something only they can perceive, embodying the Romantic idea of a beautiful world created in the artist's imagination.

The small, and to a large extent randomly formed, collection of Italian twentieth-century art is dominated by the work of modern sculptors — Greco, Manzù, Messina, Consagra — donated to the Hermitage by their creators. There are also two still lifes by Giorgio Morandi, one of the most gifted and inspired Italian artists of the century.

On one landing of the Wooden Staircase, which links the collections of recent French, German and Italian art with the Oriental Department and the Department of Russian Culture, hang four works by one of the greatest artists of the twentieth century, Wassily Kandinsky (1866–1944). He was born

André Derain
Grove. Ca. 1912

56

Caspar David Friedrich
On a Sailing-Ship. 1818–19

and grew up in Russia, spent his best creative years in Germany, but died and is buried in France. His paintings are without nationality; they are a part of twentieth-century world art. These Kandinsky paintings, which include one of his acknowledged masterpieces, the monumental *Composition No 6* (1915), came into the Hermitage in 1948 after the closure of the State Museum of New Western Art in Moscow.

In the south-western part of the palace a set of living apartments has survived that were created for the marriage of the future Emperor Alexander II, then heir to the throne. The decoration of these rooms began at the same time as the work to restore the Winter Palace after the great fire and was finished by April 1841.

The "new suite of the heir", as it was known, consisted of the apartments of his bride Maria Alexandrovna. The main state room of this suite was the White Hall created by Alexander Briullov. The architect found a superb solution for this huge hall with two tiers of windows decorated in shades of white. The moulded ornament included depictions of military trophies, mythological figures and scenes. Besides that, the hall was adorned by *bas-reliefs* of Jupiter and Juno, Apollo and Diana, Mercury and Ceres, Neptune and Vesta.

The adjoining Golden Drawing-Room was intended by Briullov as a contrast

The main imperial residence in Russia had an exceptionally broad range of functions. For a century and a half, the palace was the centre of political and ceremonial life, not only for St Petersburg, but for the empire as a whole: the focus of social and cultural events in the city. It was the setting for official rituals, festive religious services, balls, plays and concerts. The palace was home to the imperial family, their immediate retinue, and a huge staff. It was a tremendous household with an enormous number of kitchens, storerooms, ice-boxes, stoves and fireplaces — and, to keep it all going, an army of servants, cooks, stokers, tailors and seamstresses. The palace was sub-divided into sets of rooms connected by location, common purpose or occupation by a particular person, and a certain style of architectural decoration. Each of these sets of apartments could be allocated to any function, but, although the occupier or decoration might change, their boundaries rarely did. When the palace was restored after the 1837 fire, living apartments were created for Emperor Nicholas I, Empress Alexandra Fiodorovna, the heir to the throne, other grand dukes and duchesses, and the Minister of the Imperial Court, as well as several "reserve sets of apartments" for exalted visitors and more distant relatives of the Tsar.

to the White Hall. The decoration of this room, according to the architect's concept, was supposed to form a sort of pair with the main drawing-room of Empress Alexandra Fiodorovna (wife of Nicholas I) — the Malachite Room, that was also called "golden" in the nineteenth century. In the Golden Drawing-Room of Maria Alexandrovna the walls and vault were originally covered in white artificial marble with only the delicate moulded ornament being gilded. The furniture was completely gilded; the panels painted in imitation of lapis lazuli, a deep blue semiprecious stone. The interior was completed by a marble fireplace decorated with a *bas-relief* and a mosaic picture framed by jasper columns. In the 1860s–70s the walls here were completely gilded over.

The Golden Drawing-Room now contains showcases for a unique collection of cameos and intaglios made by skilled Western European craftsmen from semiprecious stones with layers of different colours — cornelian, agate,

The White Hall

chalcedony, amethyst and onyx. This is one of the largest collections in Europe. It was started by Catherine the Great who described her passion for such stones as a disease. In a brief span of time she bought the collections of the Duc d'Orléans, de Breteuil and Casanova which as well as highly valuable examples of European glyptic art also included works by ancient gem-cutters. Some of the cameos were produced in the workshop of the Browns, celebrated English craftsmen, to Catherine's personal commission.

As well as the state rooms, the private living quarters of Maria Alexandrovna — the Crimson Study, Boudoir, Blue Bedroom, Bathroom, Lavatory and Green Dining-Room — have retained their decoration.

*Apollo Slaying Python
Cameo. 16th century
Milan, Italy. By Alessandro
Masnago. Agate*

Of particular interest in the west wing are the interiors that in the nineteenth century were regarded as memorial rooms. These rooms overlooking the Admiralty were decorated by Quarenghi in 1791 for Catherine's eldest grandson the future Alexander I. In 1793 the rooms were vacated as after his marriage Alexander and his bride lived in another part of the palace. Alexander's brother Konstantin lived in the apartments for three years, until his marriage, when they passed to the next brother, Nicholas. When he became Emperor, Nicholas I decided to continue the tradition and gave the rooms to his heir, the future Alexander II. Because of the special associations of these apartments in which three Russian monarchs grew up, their style of decoration was never changed. After the fire Briullov reproduced the interiors here "down to the last detail".

One of the most exquisite is the Boudoir. Briullov's 1841 decoration of the room was completely replaced in 1853 by Harald Bosse in keeping with a new vogue for the Rococo style with delicate carved and gilded motifs, and virtuoso painted insets in the walls and ceiling. The architect used paintings from the Hermitage stocks as decoration above the doors. The Boudoir is given a special sense of intimacy by a sort of alcove, separated by a step, a low gilded railing and drapes. The architect originally wanted to stress this division by colour too, lining the walls of the alcove in white, and the rest of the Boudoir in crimson fabric. The deep red material used for the wall panels, upholstery and drapes for the windows and doors was commissioned from the Cortier factory in France.

After the fire, rooms in the western wing of the Winter Palace that adjoins Maria Alexandrovna's apartments were allocated to the sons of Nicholas I — the heir to the throne Grand Duke Alexander (the future Alexander II) and his brothers, Konstantin, Nikolai and Mikhail.

The Emperor's own apartments were separated from those of the Grand Dukes by the long, narrow Dark Corridor — a service room in which guardsmen were on duty. Until the 1917 revolution its walls were hung with silver trays for offering bread and salt — the traditional Russian welcome ceremony — that were given to the Russian Emperors as mementoes of formal meetings with their subjects. From July 1917 the western part of the Winter Palace served as the residence of the Provisional Government. The Dark Corridor linked the reception rooms and offices of Prime Minister Alexander Kerensky with the clerks' offices. It was here that the historic storm of the Winter Palace took place. On the night of 24 October (7 November New Style) 1917

The Boudoir

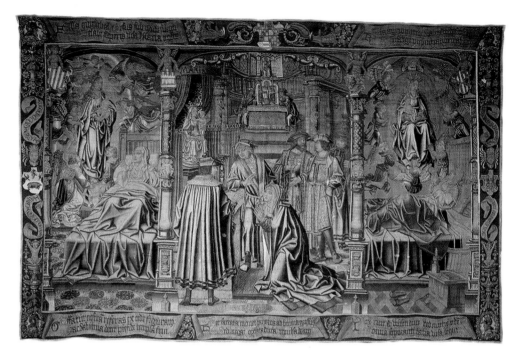

The Appearance of the Madonna. Tapestry from the Appearance of the Sablon Madonna series. From a cartoon by Bernard van Orley. 1518–19 Brussels, Flanders Wool, silk

Proof of an Emperor Konstantin rouble. 1825 Russia. Silver

After the death of Alexander I on 27 November 1825, the throne should have passed to his eldest brother Grand Duke Konstantin. The Ministry of Finance began to prepare for the minting of new coins with the portrait of the new Emperor. Konstantin abdicated, however, in favour of the next brother, Nicholas, who became Emperor Nicholas I on 14 December 1825. The proof Emperor Konstantin coins were kept in the stores of the Ministry of Finance. In 1878 Alexander II distributed five silver roubles among collectors; one of them is now in the Numismatic Department of the Hermitage.

detachments of revolutionary soldiers and sailors entered the palace through "His Imperial Majesty's Entrance" (now the October Entrance) and made their way along the Dark Corridor to the Malachite Room which was being used for cabinet meetings. They arrested the Provisional Government and opened the way to the declaration of Soviet power.

Today the walls of the Dark Corridor are adorned with Western European tapestries of the seventeenth and eighteenth centuries. The Hermitage possesses an extremely rich collection of tapestries which are reminiscent of monumental painted panels in the complexity of their compositions and the wealth of different colours. The production of tapestries is an exceptionally difficult and painstaking business: in the course of a year an experienced craftsman could weave no more than one to one and a half square metres (11–16 square feet) of a picture.

At the present time, the western part of the Winter Palace houses the Departments of Numismatics, Oriental and Russian Culture.

The Department of Russian Culture is the youngest in the Hermitage, having been established just before the Nazi invasion of the Soviet Union in 1941. The name derives from a special selection of exhibits that illustrate the history, culture and daily life of the Russian state from ancient times to the twentieth century. In the halls of the museum visitors can see a relatively small, but first-rate collection of Early Russian icons and fragments of frescoes, as well as the work of potters, weavers, the weapon-smiths of Tula and the ivory carvers of the North. And the Winter Palace itself, the architectural decoration of its rooms, the furniture, chandeliers, parquet floors and vases — all the remarkable complex created by the efforts of numerous architects, artists and craftsmen — is the priceless exhibit of this department.

The pride of the Hermitage collection are items from the time of Peter the Great. The core of them belong to the "Study of Peter the Great" that was kept in the Kunstkammer from the eighteenth century. In 1848–49 the exhibits in that study were transferred to the Winter Palace where a "Gallery of Peter

the Great" was formed. We can judge about the great transformations brought about in Russia by Peter from the set of lathes designed by Andrei Nartov for the Tsar's own workshop, measuring instruments that Peter used, portraits of his companions-in-arms and contemporaries by Ivan Nikitin, Andrei Matveyev, Luigi Caravaque and Johann Tannauer, engravings of St Petersburg by Alexei Zubov. Among the finest works of sculpture produced in Russia are bronze busts of Peter and Prince Alexander Menshikov created by the Italian Bartolommeo Carlo Rastrelli (1675–1744) who was invited to Russia for three years by the Tsar but stayed the rest of his life. Rastrelli, father of the architect, also created the famous life-size wax figure of Peter the Great commissioned by his widow Catherine I immediately after his death in 1725.

A remarkable mosaic portrait of Peter, rightly considered one of the department's finest exhibits, was created in the 1750s by Mikhail Lomonosov. That great Russian scientist, writer and artist himself revived the technique of working in smaltos, small pieces of coloured glass.

The works of Russian art from the eighteenth and nineteenth centuries that abundantly decorate the living apartments in the western part of the Winter Palace form an effective whole in combination with the rich architecture of the interiors.

Particularly luxurious are the rooms created for Empress Alexandra Fiodorovna, the wife of Nicholas I. The Malachite Room was created by Alexander Briullov in place of Montferrand's Jasper Drawing-Room. Briullov retained the originally layout of the room with the placing of the columns and pilasters around the perimeter, but at the Tsar's request, other materials were used to finish the room. "Rich Siberia replaced its jasper with gold and malachite that were also its own," a contemporary wrote. As early as the eighteenth century malachite, then a great rarity, was used in craft work: to cover table ornaments, snuffboxes, writing sets and vases.

In the 1830s, following the discovery of huge deposits of the mineral at the Demidovs' copper mines in the Urals, malachite became more extensively used. In the Empress's state drawing-room the columns and fireplaces were worked in the difficult "Russian mosaic" technique: thin plates of stone were stuck onto the base, the joints between them filled with malachite powder and the surface then polished. The combination of these elements with gilding had those who saw it in raptures, not knowing "what was more astonishing: the lavishness of the material or the lavishness of the artist's idea." The room was furnished with pieces by Heinrich Gambs and enhanced by allegorical figures representing Day, Night and Poetry.

The Malachite Room was the boundary between the state rooms and the Empress's private apartments. It provided access to the Neva Enfilade that led from the State Staircase to the Throne Room. In the 1790s, with the construction of the new throne room (St George's Hall), this suite of rooms lost its original functions and was reconstructed to a plan by Quarenghi. In place of five old rooms he created three new ones: the Concert Hall, and the Large and Small Fore-Halls, the latter giving onto the Jordan Staircase, while in the decoration the unrestrained sumptuousness of the Baroque gave way to the refined austerity of Classicism. When he restored the Neva Enfilade after the 1837 fire Stasov retained Quarenghi's layout, but made the decoration

The Malachite Room

The Small or White Dining-Room

Rooms in the north-western part of the palace were redecorated in 1894–95 for the new Emperor Nicholas II and his young bride Alexandra Fiodorovna (Princess Alix of Hesse-Darmstadt). The architect in charge of the work was Alexander Krasovsky (1848–1923). The decoration of the majority of the rooms occupied by the last Russian emperor was destroyed in the 1920s when the palace was converted for use as a museum. Only two, the dining-room and library, retained their appearance. In the White (Small) Dining-Room Krasovsky replaced Briullov's Pompeian style interior that had existed since 1839 with Rococo decoration featuring delicate moulded ornament in the form of seashells, garlands, scrolls, and the like. The furniture was produced from sketches by another architect, N. V. Nabokov. The superb stylization was complemented by authentic eighteenth-century items — tapestries produced at the St Petersburg factory (three allegorical parts of the world: *Asia*, *Africa* and *America*, and a decorative panel entitled *Swans*) and an English-made crystal chandelier. The Library of Nicholas II was stylized in the Gothic manner that was considered particularly appropriate for such purposes. The decoration of the Bremen sandstone fireplace features two heraldic beasts — the Romanov Gryphon and the Lion of Hesse, taken from the ancestral coats-of-arms of the Tsar and his spouse.

The Gothic Library of Nicholas II

of the rooms even more austere and monumental: the subtle play of superb combinations of colour in the artificial marble used to face the walls and columns was replaced by the solemn grandeur of white; minor decorative details disappeared and forms were enlarged.

The Concert Hall alongside the Malachite Room got its name from the fact that it was used for large concerts and theatrical performances. The room was decorated with depictions of the muses and Classical goddesses by the sculptor Josef Hermann and allegorical figures with attributes of the arts.

The Great Fore-Hall, the central element in the enfilade, is the largest state room in the palace. After 1856 it became known as the Nicholas Hall, as a large equestrian portrait of the Emperor by the German artist Franz Krüger was installed there following his death.

For the richness of its decoration a contemporary aptly described the (Small) Fore-Hall as "an entrance hall, but an entrance hall worthy of the imperial house". (This was the first room off the landing of the Jordan Staircase.)

Another door from the great staircase led to a different "entrance hall" of a kind — the Field Marshals' Hall. This huge room was created by Auguste Montferrand in 1833–34 and restored by Stasov in 1838–39. It was used to display portraits of Russian field marshals: Rumiantsev, Potemkin, Suvorov,

Silver Tomb of Alexander Nevsky. 1750–53
The St Petersburg Mint

This distinctive monument to the thirteenth-century Prince Alexander Nevsky, an outstanding Russian military commander and statesman, who was later canonized by the Orthodox Church, was commissioned by Empress Elizabeth. Ninety *poods* (almost one and a half tonnes) of silver — a year's output from the Kolyvan mines in the Altai — went to create it. The tomb consists of a sarcophagus decorated with reliefs of scenes from Alexander Nevsky's life and his victories over foreign invaders. This is placed against a decorative pyramid that is crowned by the coat-of-arms of the sainted prince. Two angels, on the left and right sides of the pyramid, hold cartouches engraved with texts written by Lomonosov in praise of Alexander Nevsky and Empress Elizabeth. This unique ensemble is completed by two free-standing silver trophies and two censers.

*The "Great Coach", first
quarter of the 18th century
Gobelins factory (?)
Paris, France*

This carriage was used
for coronations that
traditionally took place in
the Assumption Cathedral
of the Kremlin in Moscow.
It was acquired by Peter
the Great during his journey
abroad in 1716–17, when,
while staying in Paris, he
visited the royal Gobelins
factory. Accounts certainly
confirm that Catherine
the Great rode to
the cathedral for her
coronation in this particular
carriage. During the Second
World War the carriage was
badly damaged by shrapnel
from a shell that hit the
Winter Palace storerooms.
The thorough restoration
completed in 1991 allows
visitors to see once again an
eighteenth-century imperial
state coach in all its
luxurious splendour.

Kutuzov, Dibich and Paskevich. It acquired a certain inglorious fame from
the fact that it was here, on 17 December 1837, that the fire broke out which
ravaged the interior of the Winter Palace.

Even such a brief introduction to what is the great world of the Winter Palace
has acquainted us with several pages in the history of the Russian imperial house
and of the creation of a world-famous museum.

Leading from the Field Marshals' Hall, the Ministers' Corridor and a small
passage connect the Winter Palace with the Hermitage buildings that appeared
between the mid-eighteenth and mid-nineteenth centuries: the Small, Old and
New Hermitages and the court Hermitage Theatre, completing a celebrated
architectural masterpiece, the Hermitage palace complex.

*The Wax Figure
of Peter the Great. 1725
Bartolommeo Carlo
Rastrelli*

THE SMALL AND OLD HERMITAGES
THE HERMITAGE THEATRE

Looking along Palace Embankment, after the Baroque forms of the Winter Palace come the plainer Classical facades of several buildings with a shared historical name — the Hermitage. Constructed alongside the chief residence in the capital, the symbol of the highest authority in imperial Russia, the three Hermitages — Small, Old and New, together with the Hermitage Theatre, embodied another aspect of that authority: its intellectual and enlightened qualities.

The first foundation stone for the Hermitage was laid by Catherine the Great, who in the third year of her glorious reign resolved to have a Hanging Garden built by the Winter Palace and then, by that garden, two miniature pavilions and galleries to house her growing collections. Thus appeared the first product of Catherine's passion for building — the Small Hermitage. Conceived as a place where the Empress could withdraw into refined solitude from the fuss of ceremonial, it marked the beginning of a whole ensemble of edifices in which an empire of culture and art was born and flourished, an empire that Catherine passed on to her successors.

The decoration of the Pavilion Hall was created to the plan by Andrei Stakenschneider in 1850–58. At the same time, in the adjacent part of the Hanging Garden, the architect created a winter garden. There, around an elegant fountain, tropical plants grew casting deep emerald shadows on the white marble arcades of the Pavilion Hall. Four "fountains of tears", inspired by the original in the palace of the Crimean Khans at Bakhchisarai, raised poetic images of the Orient. Rich parquet and mosaic floors, a splendid set of chandeliers made of crystal and gilded bronze created an atmosphere of melancholy luxury in the garden. In 1939 the framework of the Winter Garden was dismantled, and now only the fountain, still occupying its former place, reminds us of it. At present the hall is used to display part of the Hermitage's collection of mosaic tables from the mid-nineteenth century and the celebrated Peacock Clock by the noted eighteenth-century English clock-maker James Cox.

*The Northern Pavilion
of the Small Hermitage*

*The Hanging Garden
of the Small Hermitage*

The Pavilion Hall

Two talented architects —Jean-Baptiste Vallin de la Mothe (1729–1800) and Yury Velten (1730–1801) — created the Small Hermitage. The former designed it, the latter skilfully made the design a reality between 1764 and 1775. Still today a wonder of the world survives here: the Hanging Garden raised on lofty vaults, laid out with paths and flower beds and decorated with pieces of sculpture. At the same time as this "upper garden" was being produced, on its southern edge Velten constructed a pavilion for the Empress's favourite, Count Grigory Orlov, and linked it by an aerial walkway to her personal apartments. This Little Palace, or Southern Pavilion as it was later called, retained its original appearance for much of its history.

Following the Southern Pavilion, a Northern, or Orangery, Pavilion appeared at the other end of the Hanging Garden in 1769. This pavilion at second-storey level contained the Orangery, a hall with two tiers of windows, five studies and the "Hermitage", a room with a table that could be raised and lowered where, undisturbed even by servants, Catherine and a select group of friends could enjoy "Small Hermitages", amusing evenings of reading, conversation, performances and games, in which the hostess and her guests participated as equals. Soon the name of these evenings became extended to the whole building. This name remained even when the pavilion was reconstructed in the middle of the nineteenth century. A special feature of the Small Hermitage are the galleries that run along three sides of the Hanging Garden. While the construction of the Orangery was still underway, Catherine herself came up with the happy idea of uniting the northern and southern pavilions with galleries that were then used to house the paintings the Empress had acquired from the Berlin merchant Johann Ernst Gotzkowsky. (This work was directed by Velten and successfully completed by 1775.) With the years the works on display in these galleries changed, and they acquired names accordingly. In the middle of the nineteenth century the western gallery became known as the Romanov Gallery, because a portrait gallery of members of Russia's ruling house was installed there. The one flanking the Hanging Garden on the south acquired the name Peter Gallery or Gallery of Views of St Petersburg; the one on the east side either the French Gallery or the Gallery of Gems and the Cabinet of Peter the Great.

Today the Southern and Romanov Galleries of the Small Hermitage contain the collections of mediaeval Western European applied art and fifteenth- and sixteenth-century painting from the Low Countries. The stock of works by old Netherlandish masters is not great, but it gives an adequate picture of artistic culture in that centre of the North European Renaissance.

Robert Campin
Madonna and Child. 1430s

The "Fortuny" Vase. 14th century. Spain

This exceptional piece of pottery, found by the artist
Mariano Fortuny near the Spanish city of Malaga in
1871, is a masterpiece of mediaeval art. The surface is
covered by a glistening bluish iridescence — the lustre
for which the works of Malaga craftsmen were
particularly famed. The vase was intended to hold
water or wine with its lower half buried in the ground.

A diptych by Robert Campin (ca. 1380–1444) — a *Madonna and Child* on the
right panel, a *Trinity* on the left — numbers among the finest works by the artist.
In his depiction of the Virgin Campin still followed the mediaeval tradition and did
not idealize her image. The painting is full of everyday objects typical for life in
the Low Countries, but every carefully and accurately painted detail here also has
a hidden meaning of religious symbolism.

Rogier van der Weyden (ca. 1400–64), a pupil of Campin, is represented in
the Hermitage collection by *St Luke Painting the Virgin.* The artist attentively and
reverently studies the beautiful, tender face of Mary, who is feeding the Christ-
Child with her breast, and the calm, concentrated figure of the apostle.
The landscape visible outside the room is an entire world crammed with vivid
details that seem to have been painted from life.

From the display of paintings representing the Netherlandish school we return

*The Hall
of the Proto-Renaissance*

In Catherine the Great's time
this was a billiard room.
Later it was converted
to house a display
of Rembrandt's paintings
and only acquired its present
appearance in the mid-
nineteenth century.
At that time, following
Stakenschneider's project,
it was turned into the State
Reception Room of
the "seventh reserve set of
apartments". The room owes
its splendour to columns
of green jasper, fireplaces,
opulent pilasters with bronze
decorations and painted
inserts. The doors are
particularly impressive.
They are made from
precious varieties of wood
and decorated with inset
oval medallions of painted
porcelain. Above the doors
are painted panels *Times
of the Day* by Michaly Zichy.

by the Romanov Gallery to the Pavilion Hall. From there we have a view through
the passageway into the interior of the next building of the complex, the Old
Hermitage. Constructed between 1770 and 1787, it was intended by the Empress
as somewhere to house her growing collections of books and works of art. With this
in mind, on the main floor of the building, on the side facing the Neva, Velten,
the architect, placed an Oval Hall that was used to house Voltaire's library and
beyond it a suite of rooms that accommodated the best works by Spanish, Italian
and Dutch artists from Catherine's collection.

*Simone Martini
The Virgin from a scene
of the Annunciation. 1330s
Right half of a diptych*

*The Nativity of Christ
15th century. Florence.
Workshop of Lucca della
Robbia. Majolica*

Three-quarters of a century later, when the New Hermitage was constructed just to the south and a large portion of the collections was transferred to that building, the function of these rooms changed. The architect Andrei Stakenschneider (1802–65) converted them into apartments for the heir to the throne. The Oval Hall was replaced with a staircase, called the Council Staircase as the Council of State met on the ground floor here, while the rooms of the picture gallery turned into state drawing-rooms, bedchambers, reception rooms and studies.

This mid-nineteenth-century setting now houses one of the most celebrated parts of the Hermitage's collections — Italian art of the fourteenth to eighteenth centuries, including masterpieces of both Renaissance and Baroque eras. That tremendous period in human history, however, produced such an immense wealth of art and artists that virtually no museum in the world can claim to possess works by all the great Italian masters of the time. The Hermitage is no exception. Noteworthy among the works of the early or Proto-Renaissance is a masterpiece

Leonardo da Vinci
*The Benois Madonna
(Madonna with a Flower)
1478*

←
The Leonardo da Vinci Hall

Originally this room housed paintings of the Spanish and Italian schools collected by Catherine the Great. In the mid-nineteenth century Stakenschneider gave the hall two tiers of windows and placed columns on tall porphyry pedestals along the side walls. In the middle of the two end walls he installed fireplaces with lapis-lazuli insets and columns covered in Russian mosaic of banded jasper. Three painted panels by the seventeenth-century Venetian artist Padovanino have survived in the room since Catherine's time. The doors are exceptional, being finished in the brass-and-tortoiseshell Boulle technique. A reminder of the hall's use as a state room are six relief portraits of outstanding Russian military commanders: Suvorov, Kutuzov, Rumiantsev, Potemkin, Paskevich and Dolgorukov.

*Boulle-technique doors in
the Leonardo da Vinci Hall*

created by the fourteenth-century Sienese master Simone Martini (1283–1344) — the Virgin from a scene of the *Annunciation*. The painting is the right half of a diptych. (The left half depicting the Archangel Gabriel is in the National Gallery, Washington.)

One of the greatest artists of the fifteenth century, Fra Beato Angelico da Fiesole (ca. 1400–55) took monastic vows and for practically his entire career worked to commissions from religious houses. In the 1420s he executed a series of frescoes for a monastery at Fiesole near Florence. In the nineteenth century the monastery was closed and the precious wall-paintings by Fra Angelico cut up into sections and sold. *The Madonna and Child with St Dominic and St Thomas Aquinas*, the central part of the composition, came into the Hermitage in 1883. This depiction of the Madonna enthroned with saints at the sides derives from mediaeval tradition and is known as the *Sacra Conversazione* ("Holy Conversation"), but here

Leonardo da Vinci
The Litta Madonna
Early 1480s

the artist has given the saints a more earthly appearance.

The name of the fifteenth-century Florentine master Lucca della Robbia (1400–82) is associated with the use of majolica — tin-glazed earthenware — to create sculptural reliefs, portraits, and multi-figure compositions that often adorned the walls of luxurious *palazzi*. We can get some idea of della Robbia's style from the relief of *The Nativity of Christ* produced in his workshop.

Dating from the High Renaissance, the period when Italian art reached its loftiest heights, are two paintings by Leonardo da Vinci, the same number by Raphael and Giorgione, nine works by Titian, and a sculpture by Michelangelo.

The *Benois Madonna* (*Madonna with a Flower*) by Leonardo da Vinci (1452–1519) is among the earliest works by this artistic genius. The painting came into

Titian. Danaë
Between 1546 and 1553

Titian did not stick strictly
to the details of the myth:
his Danaë is seen not in
a tower but against
a landscape. The servant
looks like an authentic aged
Venetian woman, while
Zeus, whose face can be seen
among the clouds, appears
to his beloved in the form
of a shower of gold coins.
The elemental forces
of nature and human
emotions merge in a single
spontaneous outburst.

the Hermitage at the beginning of the twentieth century from the collection
of the Russian architect Leonty Benois. It was executed in 1478 in oils, a technique
that originated in the Netherlands and rarely used in Italy at the time. Leonardo has
treated the traditional subject almost as a genre scene: the image of the Virgin is far
from the ideal, there is nothing divine about it; this is rather a young Florentine
woman playing with her child. The figures are given special weight, balance and
elevated significance by the two sources of light from the side and the back.

The same qualities are also present in full measure in another masterpiece by
Leonardo the *Litta Madonna* which came from the collection of the Milanese Duke
of Litta. The stable composition, pithiness, almost mathematically attuned details
and harmonious choice of colours do not obscure the subtle psychological resonance
of the image — the gaze of a mother, full of tenderness, thoughtful and sad, as if
with a premonition of her son's future sufferings.
The painting would seem to have more traditional details than the *Benois Madonna*
— the red and blue colour of the Virgin's clothing, the bird in the hand of
the Christ-Child, symbolizing the spilt blood of the Saviour, but the ideal that
the artist created became one of the greatest achievements of the High Renaissance.

Venice, the "Pearl of the Adriatic", made a significant contribution to the history
of Italian painting. The very appearance of this splendid city, seeming to glitter with
precious shades of colour, encouraged the emergence here of celebrated masters of
colour. The High Renaissance opened in Venice with the name of Giorgione (Giorgio
de Castelfranco; ca. 1478–1510). Despite his brief life (the artist died at the age
of 33 during a plague epidemic), Giorgione played a decisive role in the
development of Venetian painting. *Judith* is among the generally acknowledged
masterpieces of the Hermitage collection. Giorgione tackled the then popular theme

of a heroic deed as the worthiest expression of human nature in the image of a beautiful young woman against a background of a bright landscape. Even the head of the Assyrian general Holofernes lying at Judith's feet and the sword in her hand do not disturb the sense of calm and purity that emanates from the figure of this heroine of the apocryphal story.

The peak of Venetian art in the Renaissance period is justly regarded as being the painting of Giorgione's pupil Titian (1485/90–1576). The best known works by the artist in the Hermitage were created towards the end of his long life. Titian tackled the story of *Danaë* on several occasion: the widespread use of Classical myths in this period was bound up with an aesthetic conception that originated in the Ancient World and held that the naked human body was the most

Titian. The Repentant Mary Magdalene. 1560s

The Hermitage Theatre

*The auditorium of
the Hermitage Theatre*

An additional attraction
of the Hermitage Theatre
is the memorial exhibition
of the Winter Palace of Peter
the Great. It was created
in the lower storey very
recently, in the second half
of the 1980s, during the
reconstruction of the theatre.
Archaeological excavations
uncovered architectural
fragments of a palace erected
in the late 1710s and 1720s.
Quarenghi had preserved
them in the foundation of his
building and so provided
the opportunity two hundred
years later to recreate part
of the courtyard, a gallery
with a striking arcade and
some of the interiors of the
Winter Palace of the city's
founder. And so two
historical eras now co-exist
in the Hermitage Theatre,
permeated with the spirit
of two great rulers, Peter
and Catherine.

beautiful creation of Nature. The proportions of the naked body of Titian's Danaë
have something in common with the beauty of ancient statues, but they are infused
with life by the mighty brush of the great sixteenth-century Venetian.

The Repentant Mary Magdalene is another of Titian's masterpieces.
The beautiful sinner, presented in the act of unrestrained, impassioned repentance
seems to have been woven from a wealth of glittering strokes of paint, glistening
with deep shades of colour.

The extensive display of Italian fourteenth- to sixteenth-century art occupies
all the main floor of the Old Hermitage building and ends at the meeting-point of
the Theatre Staircase, the Raphael Loggias and the foyer of the Hermitage Theatre.
At this point a striking "Venetian arch" thrown across the Winter Canal links
the Hermitage buildings with one of the most exquisite components of the former
imperial residence — the Hermitage Theatre. The decree ordering its construction
was signed by Catherine the Great on 6 November 1783. Two years later, on 16
November 1785, an entry was made in the court journal reporting that the Empress
and members of the imperial family "proceeded through the Hermitage to the new
theatre where they watched the rehearsal of a comic opera..." The designer, and
constructor within such a short period, of the new building was the noted Italian-
born St Petersburg architect Giacomo Quarenghi. He has the honour of having
created on the bank of the Neva a true masterpiece that became one of the finest
palace theatres in Russia and indeed in Europe. The harmony and clarity of
the Hermitage Theatre mark it out in the panorama of Palace Embankment, and
it completes in a style "as exquisite as all the rest" the ensemble of Hermitage
buildings. Behind the Classical façade of the building, which is particularly striking
when viewed from the junction of the Neva and the Winter Canal, the architect
installed a magnificent auditorium and stage. Taking his lead from Ancient Roman
prototypes, Quarenghi designed the interior in the form of an amphitheatre and
with his inherent sense of proportion decorated the proscenium arch and the walls
with Corinthian semi-columns and niches, enriching the auditorium with sculpture
in the form of heavenly and earthly gods of the theatre. The Hermitage Theatre
played host to the finest Russian and foreign companies. It witnessed the brilliant
talents of Ivan Dmitrevsky, Vera Samoilova, Fiodor Chaliapin, Mathilda Ksches-
sinska and many other outstanding actors, singers and ballet dancers of the
eighteenth to twentieth centuries. Still today the Hermitage Theatre retains for
the most part its original appearance which splendidly combines the elegance
and sense of intimacy proper to the private theatre of the imperial family.

THE NEW HERMITAGE

The New Hermitage holds a unique place in the architectural complex of museum buildings. It appeared at the behest of Nicholas I who recognised the necessity of constructing a special building capable of accommodating the art treasures belonging to the crown that were then scattered around the many palaces in the capital. The Tsar commissioned the plans for the "Imperial Museum" from the court architect of King Ludwig I of Bavaria, Leo von Klenze, who in collaboration with his Russian colleagues Vasily Stasov, Nikolai Yefimov and Alexander Briullov created a unique work of architecture.

The Raphael Loggias

Dish. 16th century
Deruta, Italy. Majolica

The Hermitage has some
500 examples of Italian
Renaissance majolica —
magnificent and extremely
expensive dishes, vessels
and wine-coolers. They were
made of earthenware
covered with an opaque
glaze, painted with bright
colours and then fired again.
These highly prized
collector's items often
feature reproductions
of works by famous artists,
including Raphael. In Italy
there were several noted
centres producing majolica,
whose products differed in
certain distinctive features.
In Deruta, for example,
majolica dishes were given
a very thin lustrous
overglaze that gave the piece
an iridescent metallic sheen.
The formula for this
overglaze was a carefully
guarded secret.

The Majolica Hall

The New Hermitage was an embodiment of the age's conception of the museum as a universal repository of the artistic experience of mankind. This idea determined the architectural structure of the New Hermitage, the first purpose-built museum in Russia. It even determined the decoration of the façades, for which von Klenze choose the Neo-Grecian style deriving ultimately from Ancient Greece. In keeping with the Emperor's wishes, all the halls of the museum, irrespective of the character of the items displayed, were decorated in a grand manner befitting the royal residence of which they formed a part. The lower storey of the building was allotted to the exhibition of ancient and modern sculpture, while the upper storey was mainly occupied by the collections of paintings belonging to the court. Everything was organized in a particular manner with the sole aim of compiling a universal, encyclopaedic picture of the history of world art. A museum within a museum, that is what the New Hermitage remains to this day, presenting a single cultural universe. Here different genres and art forms co-exist in surprising harmony. One of the most impressive is the Raphael Loggias ensemble, created in 1783–92 to satisfy the ambitious aspirations of Catherine the Great and incorporated into the Museum by von Klenze half a century later. These superb copies of Raphael's frescoes (now all but lost) and their setting in the Vatican found a highly worthy place among the elaborate interiors of the New Hermitage.

Original works by the great Renaissance artist are displayed in the adjoining Majolica Hall. There, surrounded by colourful examples of Italian ceramic art from the sixteenth century, visitors can admire two painted masterpieces by Raphael (Raffaello Santi; 1483–1520).

The story of St Petersburg's Raphael Loggias is unique. In the late 1770s Catherine the Great commissioned copies of the famous frescoes executed by Raphael and his pupils in 1516–18 in the loggias of the Vatican Palace. The copies, made in egg tempera on canvas, were made by a team of artists led by Christoph Unterberger. A year later the architect Quarenghi arrived at the Russian court for the purpose of installing the copies in Catherine's winter residence. The careful measurements of the Vatican loggias that he made before leaving for Russia determined the choice of a site for the new extension. In 1783 work began on the construction of the gallery next to the (Old) Hermitage, alongside the Winter Canal. Eleven year later the works that have preserved the appearance of Raphael's unique creation were installed there. Half a century on, when the New Hermitage was built, the Raphael Loggias block was partially reconstructed so that its interior with the whole painted ensemble was incorporated into the museum building. And so, this great work of art that has been called "Raphael's Bible" enjoyed a second rebirth in the Hermitage.

Michelangelo
Crouching Boy. 1530s
Marble

The Michelangelo Room

The Michelangelo Room, now used to display the great master's *Crouching Boy*, is the last in the series of "Cabinets of Small Italian Painting". Situated alongside the Large Skylight Hall, it originally served as a place for Nicholas I's wife, Empress Alexandra Fiodorovna, to rest during her long strolls around the New Hermitage. The room was finished with regal refinement which subtly combined white marble walls with gilded furniture and mouldings and an elegantly patterned parquet floor. The exhibits here consisted of the astonishing collection of ancient gold artefacts found in the vicinity of Kerch in the eastern Crimea. On the walls are frescoes that were painted by pupils of Raphael.

The *Conestabile Madonna* was considered the gem of the collection held by Count Conestabile in Perugia, where the artist was born. The decision to sell the work abroad raised such a storm of protest among the Italians that the Count, who was badly in need of money, was obliged to publish a special brochure explaining his reasons. The relatively small work is a *tondo*, a round painting. A young Virgin of exquisite beauty holding the Christ-Child with a book in her lap, is placed against the background of a panoramic landscape. The soft line of the hills, the mirror surface of the lake, the slender trees covered with light spring foliage — this poetic, entirely harmonious landscape is reminiscent of Umbria, the artist's native region. The picture is set in a sumptuous gilded frame that once formed a single whole with the image as it was carved from the same wooden panel (according to legend following a sketch by the artist himself) on which the work was painted. After this precious purchase arrived in the Hermitage in 1871, specialists discovered that cracks in the wooden base of the painting had grown and it was decided to carry out a difficult restoration operation — transferring the painting to canvas.

In 1504 Raphael moved from Perugia to Florence where the second Hermitage painting, *The Madonna with the Beardless Joseph*, was painted.

Practically all the finest works of Michelangelo (1475–1564), one of the greatest of the Renaissance titans, are in Italy. This brilliant painter, sculptor and architect is represented outside his homeland only by a few works. The *Crouching Boy* sculpture is the only work by Michelangelo in the Hermitage. The light alternately flares up and dies on the rough piece of marble, as if stressing the tension that fills the compressed figure of the young man. Not the face, barely chiselled out, but the body with the muscles of the back and legs protruding powerfully, a compressed spring ready to straighten out, but pushed down seemingly by an unbearable weight, reveals the sculptor's concept.

At its basis lie the tragic reflections of the artist on a world that no longer has room for harmony and beauty.

It is believed that this sculpture was originally one of the decorative figures devised by Michelangelo to decorate the family mausoleum of the Medici rulers of Florence. One of the sketches for the decoration of the burial chapel does indeed contain depictions of crouching boys, placed at the top in niches above the tomb, that are reminiscent of the Hermitage statue. The artist seems to have later modified his concept, however, and the *Crouching Boy* was executed as a work in its own right. The statue looks unfinished, but scholars of Michelangelo's work are divided over whether the great sculptor did indeed abandon the piece, leaving the marble unpolished, or this was a consciously chosen method. The surface of the sculptor's later creations often look "churned up", something which gives them a special inner dynamism and drama.

The art of Michelangelo was the culmination of the Renaissance — the greatest stage in the history of art in the Modern Age.

Small rooms in the New Hermitage known as Cabinets, as well as the Large and Small Italian Skylight Halls contain works by Italian artists of the late sixteenth to eighteenth centuries. The peculiarities of the Late Renaissance in Venice are revealed in the monumental canvases by the followers of Titian:

The Spanish Skylight Hall Torchère. 1805. Designed by Andrei Voronikhin Kolyvan Lapidary Works

The Small Italian Skylight Hall

The three large interconnected halls in the heart of the New Hermitage are known as the Skylight Halls. The name comes from the fact that they are lit from above through massive glazed areas in the ceiling. These tremendous rooms were specially designed by the architect to accommodate the monumental canvases produced by the Italian and Spanish schools between the late sixteenth and eighteenth centuries. A notable feature of the decorations in these rooms are items made of malachite, porphyry and lapis-lazuli. These vases, table-tops and torchères were produced at the Peterhof, Yekaterinburg and Kolyvan Lapidary Works.

Caravaggio
The Lute-Player. Ca. 1595

Paolo Veronese, Tintoretto, Jacopo Bassano, Jacopo Palma the Younger, hanging
in the Small Skylight Hall. The Hermitage collection covers all the chief trends
in Italian seventeenth-century art, including superb examples of work by
the founders of the Bologna Academy, which became the prototype for such
institutions around the world: the brothers Annibale and Lodovico Carracci,
Guido Reni, Domenico, and Guercino. Among the Hermitage's masterpieces is
its sole work by Caravaggio (Michelangelo Merisi da Caravaggio; 1571–1610).
Caravaggio was the father of a powerful realistic tendency in seventeenth-century
art, one of the forerunners of the Baroque. The influence of his painting on
contemporaries can only be compared with that of the great Renaissance figures
on their age. Caravaggio had devoted followers in other European countries:
France, Spain, Holland and Flanders. *The Lute-Player* vividly reveals
the innovative achievements of Caravaggio's art. By a deliberate heightening of
the contrasts between light and shade, the artist attains an extreme sense of
volume, an almost illusory materiality or sculptural quality in the painted form.
The beautiful, soft face of the young musician, delicate, almost feminine hands
and the soft lines of neck and shoulders stress the individuality of the model,
while the fruit, sheet music, bouquet of flowers, violin and bow on the table have
been painted with precision and verisimilitude. Yet this seemingly simple genre
scene has a concealed allegorical message. Beauty and youth are soon lost: this
is hinted at by the broken string on the bow and the crack in the table-top.

In the eighteenth century only the Venetian school continued to uphold the fame

of Italian art. A pride of the Hermitage collection are works by the celebrated monumental artist and brilliant colourist Giovanni Battista Tiepolo, the landscape painters Antonio Canale and Francesco Guardi.

Eternally festive and beautiful as in a dream — that is how the lagoon city

The Knights' Hall

The room now known as the Knights' Hall was created to display the imperial numismatic collection. The small-scale nature of the exhibits enabled von Klenze to introduce rich painted ornament in the decoration of the walls and ceiling, as well as panels of artificial marble. The painting was executed by Johann Drollinger and Daniel Jensen. After the collection of Western European arms and armour of the fifteenth to seventeenth centuries was moved here, the room acquired its present name.

Jacob Jordaens
The Bean King. Ca. 1638

The subject of this painting
is the traditional festive meal
at Epiphany, or the Feast of
the Magi (6 January). An old
Dutch tradition called for
a pie with a bean baked into
it to be served on that day
and whoever found the bean
in his portion became
"the King of the Feast".

appears in *The Reception of the French Ambassador in Venice* by the virtuoso
Antonio Canale (1697–1768), known as Canaletto. At the same time every element
here is accurate, as is the historical event depicted. Venetian painters created
a special type of architectural landscape marked by an almost photographic
precision in the depiction of details, yet in their pictures the city remains full
of the charm and mystery that still make it attractive today.

Two mighty and independent artistic centres — Holland and Flanders —
emerged in Europe in the early seventeenth century. In the Hermitage they are
represented by a collection of exceptionally quality and richness that contains
paintings by almost all the leading artists of the century, that was the highest
point in the history of these national schools.

Flemish painting s distinguished by a rare monolithic quality. In essence,
its character and achievements were entirely determined by the work of the head
of the school — Peter Paul Rubens (1577–1640). All Flemish artists were to
one degree or another influenced by that great figure. Rubens' studio tackled
anything and everything: painting from monumental decorative panels to
landscapes and portraits, sculpture, architecture, applied art and was considered
a real academy of art. Rubens established the life-affirming character of Flemish
art that is founded on a rich colour scheme, temperamental dynamic movement
and materially solid forms. *The Bean King* was created by Jacob Jordaens
(1593–1678), a master of genre painting.

In the work of Frans Snyders (1579–1657) the still life lost its intimate quality
and became a monumental, dynamic celebration of the abundance of natural
forms. *The Game Shop* is one of a series of four paintings commissioned for
the Bishop of Bruges's dining-room.

A brilliant portrait painter sought by many including European monarchs,

The Snyders Hall

The Snyders Hall

According to the original project, the Snyders Hall was to be used for a display of ancient medals and coins. Shortly before the opening of the New Hermitage, however, it was decided that large paintings by Russian artists would be hung in the room. At that point all the walls were lined with crimson cloth, completely covering the painted decoration. The display of Russian paintings remained in the room until 1897 when they were transferred to the new Russian Museum. Later seventeenth-century Flemish paintings were installed here, including the still lifes by Frans Snyders, whose name the room now bears.

Anthony van Dyck (1599–1641) is represented in the Hermitage by more than twenty works. The artist's virtuoso *Self-Portrait* is full of refined artistry.

Rubens' own *Union of Earth and Water* (ca. 1618) is a work painted with

Frans Snyders
The Game Shop. 1609

Peter Paul Rubens
Perseus and Andromeda
Early 1620s

The collection of works
by Rubens numbers more
than forty items: monu-
mental canvases on biblical
and mythological subjects,
portraits, sketches
for the embellishment
of architectural structures
and the frescoing of palaces.
Virtually every one is
reckoned among
the masterpieces
of the great Flemish artist.

Anthony van Dyck
Self-Portrait
Late 1620s — early 1630s

Peter Paul Rubens
The Union of Earth
and Water
Between 1612 and 1615

a dynamic, expansive freedom. It is an allegory in which the Earth goddess
Cybele represents Flanders and her union with Neptune, the god of the sea,
indicates the need to obtain access to the sea for the country to flourish.

The main customers for the works of Dutch painters in the seventeenth
century were wealthy burghers who decorated their homes with depictions
of daily existence, still lifes, portraits, and landscapes that were generally
of no great size. It has therefore become customary to refer to their painters

Willem Claesz Heda
Breakfast. 1648

as "the small Dutch masters". These artists painted accurately and subtly, not prettifying but poeticizing the lives and daily round of their upright, sober-minded fellow citizens. Willem Claesz Heda (1594– between 1680 and 1682) created a realm of astonishing beauty and harmony from everyday objects. In *A Glass of Lemonade* Gerard Ter Borch (1617–81) turned a scene of procurement into a refined world glowing with precious shades of colour. *The Revellers* by Jan Steen (1626–79) is full of humour and secretive, sly allusions. In *Portrait of a Young Man* the outstanding portrait-painter Frans Hals (1581/85–1666) seems to have captured a fleeting image in rapid motion.

The peak of Dutch painting comes in the work of one of the seventeenth century's greatest artists: Rembrandt van Rijn (1606–69). The Hermitage possesses a priceless collection of over twenty paintings reflecting all stages of his dramatic career. *Flora* (1634) is a poetic depiction of Rembrandt's wife Saskia in the guise of the goddess of flowers and gardens. The artist is clearly feasting his eyes on his young spouse, dressing here in a luxurious festive dress and adorning her head with a wreath of flowers. In this happy time the artist was rich, loved and celebrated. Soon, however, Saskia died and that loss was followed by the gradual demise of wealth and fame. *Danaë*, a masterpiece completed after Saskia's death, lets us sense the cause of the conflict between the great artist

Frans Hals
Portrait of a Young
Man with a Glove
1660s

Jan Steen
Revellers. Ca. 1660

Gerard Ter Borch
A Glass of Lemonade. 1660s

*Rembrandt. The Return
of the Prodigal Son
Late 1660s*

The 15 June 1985 was very nearly the last day in the existence of this masterpiece by the great Dutch artist «Danaë». The painting was splashed with sulphuric acid and slashed twice with a knife. Specialist restorers urgently summoned to the Rembrandt Hall found some places on the canvas a bubbling brown mass. The painstaking restoration of this priceless work lasted about ten years. The restorers reinforced the surviving authentic layer of the painting and carefully toned in the damaged areas with a layer of paint close to Rembrandt's painted surface, entirely resisting the temptation to reconstruct Rembrandt's manner of painting. Now the work has returned to its public in the Hermitage.

and society. His works were too complex, too deep and psychological to be understood and properly appreciated by his contemporaries. *The Return of the Prodigal Son* draws the final balance of Rembrandt's life, as it were — the artist left alone, stripped of all earthly pleasures apart from the great capacity to create. The emotions that pervade all Rembrandt's work — love, suffering, forgiveness — here reach their greatest intensity.

The Golden Age of Spanish Art is customarily taken to be the seventeenth century, but it began as far back as the 1570s with Domenico Theotocopulos (1541–1614), a Greek-born artist who moved to Spain and became known as El Greco. The Hermitage canvas *The Apostles Peter and Paul* was the first

*Rembrandt. Portrait of
Saskia in the Guise of Flora
1634*

Rembrandt. Danaë. 1636

Francesco de Zurbarán
The Girlhood of the Virgin
Ca. 1660

Diego Velázquez
Breakfast. Ca. 1617—18

of the *apostolados* series created in Toledo, works devoted to Christ and
the twelve apostles. In a highly expressive manner —through colour, rhythm
and movement — El Greco contrasts the highly dissimilar followers of Christ:
Peter soft, wavering, full of doubt, and Paul certain that he is right and
fanatically dedicated to Christian ideas.

Among the greatest achievements of Spanish art in the seventeenth century
are the works of Diego Velazquez, Jose de Ribera, Francisco de Zurbarán and
Bartolomé Esteban Murillo. The oeuvre of Velázquez (1599–1660), the country's
leading artist, court painter to King Philip IV, is represented in the Hermitage
by two paintings. *Breakfast* by the eighteenth-year-old painter belongs to the
bodegón genre that was exceptionally common in Spain and undoubtedly testifies
to an enthusiasm for the work of Caravaggio. A *bodegón* (from the Spanish for
"tavern") was usually an inn scene with typically Spanish figures sitting down to
a modest meal, lit by a narrowly directed "Caravaggist" light that picks them out,
as it were, from the semidarkness of the background. As with Caravaggio himself,
this overtly humdrum subject in fact has several layers of meaning. The elements
of the foreground still life —pomegranate, bread and glass of wine — are
Christian symbols, while the boy, young man and old man were connected with
the idea of the three periods in human life.

The artistic career of Francisco de Zurbarán (1598–1664) unfolded in the
Andalusian capital Seville, a major cultural centre for the country. His paintings
on religious subjects adorned the walls of many Sevillian churches and religious
houses. Only a small number of works by this distinctive Spanish artist can be
found outside his homeland. The Hermitage collection includes four of them.

The Girlhood of the Virgin is one of the few intimate lyrical works from the brush of this usually austere and outwardly emotionally restrained master. Mary — a black-haired, dark-eyed Spanish girl — lit by a powerful stream of light pouring from above seems frozen in profound prayerful ecstasy.

The works of the last master of the Golden Age, Bartolomé Esteban Murillo (1617–82) were the most popular products of Spanish painting with collectors and for that reason the Hermitage now has a significant number — seventeen, representing various periods in the artist's development. *Boy with a Dog* dates from his early period which was dominated by vivid images of little tramps,

El Greco
The Apostles Peter and Paul
Between 1587 and 1592

gypsies and beggars dressed in motley rags, but never loosing the immediacy
in the expression of feelings that is typical of their age.

The great artist Francisco Goya (1746–1828), whose work around the turn
of the nineteenth century marked the final end of the heyday of Spanish painting,
produced the *Portrait of the Actress Antonia Sarate* donated to the Hermitage
by the American collector Armand Hammer in 1974. Contemporary accounts
suggest that Doña Antonia was more noted for her beauty than her talent.
She died of consumption at the age of thirty-six and would probably have
been forgotten, were it not for two attractive, animated portraits by Goya.
The Hermitage portrait of the actress is an intimate depiction. The emotional,
moving image of a young woman — a "portrait of the heart" as one art scholar
put it — forms a kind of bridge between two eras, the parting age of great

Bartolomé Murillo
Boy with a Dog. 1650s

spiritual discoveries made by Velázquez and Rembrandt and the coming
romantic age of Delacroix, Manet, Cézanne and Picasso.

The Gallery of the History of Ancient Painting is adorned by works from two
of the most famous sculptors of the late eighteenth and early nineteenth centuries
— the Italian Antonio Canova and the Dane Bertel Thorvaldsen who worked in
Rome. In keeping with the enthusiasm for ancient art that arose in Europe in
the 1760s, the Neo-Classical statues of Canova and Thorvaldsen display a perfect
harmony of proportions and beauty of line while the surface of the stone has
been very finely worked. The collection of works by Canova (1757–1822), the last
great heir of Classical traditions in Italian art, numbers sixteen pieces. Canova
was the most popular sculptor in Europe at the start of the nineteenth century.
The best of the items in the Hermitage came from the celebrated collection

←

*The Gallery of the History
of Ancient Painting*

Lying between the Grand
Staircase and the Skylight
Halls, this room serves as a
foretaste of the Hermitage's
painted treasures. Set into
the walls are 86 paintings
telling legendary stories
of the birth of the arts
in the Ancient World.
Each was painted by Georg
Hiltensperger using pigments
mixed with hot wax on
copper plates. A special
effect is created by
the domical vaults, some
of which are crowned with
lanterns providing diffuse
lighting from above.

*Antonio Canova
The Three Graces
1813. Marble*

The Grand (Terebenin) Staircase

of Empress Josephine kept at the Malmaison Palace outside Paris.

The celebrated marble *Three Graces* was created to Josephine's commission in 1813, but the former Empress died without ever seeing it. The group, which contemporaries regarded as the finest embodiment of the new ideal of beauty, passed to Josephine's son, Prince Eugène Beauharnais, who subsequently married one of Nicholas I's daughters.

The ground-floor halls of the New Hermitage contain the collection of ancient art. This collection is divided into two parts. The first consists of works from Ancient Greece and Rome that came with various eighteenth- and nineteenth-century acquisitions; the second contains items found during excavations of Greek colonies on the northern Black Sea coast. Although rich and varied, the Hermitage collection is not evenly composed. The most precious items are the collections of Roman sculptural portraits and decorative sculpture; ancient cameos and intaglios; gold jewellery from burials in the Black Sea area; and the collection of painted vases. The valuable examples of sculpture and vases come in the main from the collection of the Italian Marchese Campana acquired at auction in Rome in 1861. As a result of immoderate spending on the purchase of ever more pieces, the Marchese, one of the greatest collectors of antiquities, ruined himself and, unable to settle his debts, was sentenced to twenty years hard labour. He had already offered his collection to Nicholas I in the 1850s, but with the chief proviso that the Tsar take it as a whole. The Hermitage did not agree to such conditions at that time; Nicholas wanted only a part of the antiquities.

*Vessel in the form of a sphinx.
5th century B.C. Phanagoria,
Black Sea coast. Painted earthenware*

*Hercules Fighting the Lion.
Roman work based on an
original created by Lysippus
in the 330s B.C. Marble*

*The Taurida Venus. Roman
copy of a Greek original
3rd century B.C. Marble*

The Dionysus Hall

Before the auction the Hermitage was accorded special rights to chose some
of the works in advance, as a result the Campana collection was divided between
Russia and France. Gedeonov, the director of the Hermitage bought about six
hundred items — more than a hundred sculptures and 500 painted vases —
paying 6,000 Italian *scudi*. That is the story behind the creation of
the Department of the Ancient World in the Hermitage.

The Dionysus Hall was specially created to house the imperial collection
of ancient sculpture. Von Klenze stylized it in imitation of an ancient gallery:
the side walls are faced with red artificial marble and divided up by massive
columns; the floor is covered with a multicoloured mosaic, while the coffered
ceiling is also authentic in type. The ancient marble sculptures are particularly
effective when seen in such an architectural setting. The hall acquired its present
name from a statue of the Ancient Greek god of wine and fertility dating from
the fourth century B.C. included in the display here.

The sculpture of Ancient Greece, like its architecture, has for all the centuries
since been considered the highest measure of beauty in art. In the Hermitage it
is mainly present in the form of Roman copies. The finest example of the ancient
ideal of beauty to be seen in the museum is reckoned to be the Taurida Venus,
based on an original of the third century B.C. — the late, Hellenistic period of
Ancient Greek art. The figure of Venus with deliberately elongated proportions, a
small, exquisite head on a long willowy neck completely accords with the ancient
ideal in which the spiritual and physical aspects are in harmonious union.

The Aura Hall

Ancient Greek statues were brightly painted, but that has been lost in
the course of time. We can obtain some idea of how they must have looked
to delighted contemporaries from the much smaller elaborately shaped
earthenware vessels from the fifth century B.C. found in a burial mound at
the site of Phanagoria, an ancient city on the Taman peninsula (to the east
of the Crimea). One vessel in the form of a sphinx is a fascinating combination
of a beautiful female face with pink skin, blue eyes and golden curls, the body
of a lion and the wings of a bird.

The collection of Greek and Roman vases contains some 15,000 items, an
undoubted masterpiece among which is the *Swallow Pelike*, a red-figure vase
attributed to a craftsman named Euphronios. It depicts a man, a youth and
a boy welcoming the appearance of the swallow as a sign that winter is over.
An inscription on the base reports their conversation. "Look, a swallow!"
the man exclaims. "Yes, by Heracles," the youth answers. "Here it is, spring,"
the boy declares.

The room known as the Jupiter Hall houses the Hermitage's best examples
of Ancient Roman sculpture. The monumental statue of the great god here is
of astonishing size. It dates from the first century B.C. and was discovered during
excavations of a temple near Rome. Soon it was offered to Catherine the Great,
through middle-men, but she suspected fraud and declined. Nevertheless
the statue was destined to find its way to the Hermitage, arriving as part
of the Campana collection.

Statues like this one were created for many temples of Jupiter, the highest
deity in the Roman pantheon. Ancient accounts suggest that the first depiction of
Zeus (the Greek equivalent) in the form of a powerful, well-built, handsome man
seated on a throne with a small figure of Nike, the goddess of victory, in one hand

*Portrait of a Roman
1st century B.C. Rome
Bronze*

The creator of this bust
has become known as
"the sculptor of the
Leningrad bronze", proof
of the high quality of this
work from the period when
the tradition of the Roman
sculptural portrait was
only forming.

The Kolyvan Vase Hall

Originally this hall was
intended for a display of
modern sculpture. In 1850,
however, while the New
Hermitage was still being
built, a unique green jasper
vase was installed here.
It was made at the Kolyvan
Lapidary Works to the design
of the architect Avram
Melnikov. Siberian stone-
cutters worked fourteen
years to produce the vase
from a single block weighing
nineteenth tonnes. It was
delivered to St Petersburg
on carts drawn by about
160 horses.

The Jupiter Hall

*Jupiter. Late 1st century
Marble*

The interior here reproduces
the inside of an ancient
temple. The space is divided
into three aisles by two
rows of Ionic columns made
from Serdobol granite.
The original name
of the room — the Hall
of Greek and Etruscan Vases
— indicates the display
which the decoration was
intended to suit. The walls
feature motifs stylized in
imitation of the painting
on ancient lacquered vases.
They were created by the
painters Fiodor Wunderlich
and Piotr Shamshin.
The unique mosaic floor
was produced at the Peterhof
Lapidary Works.

and a sceptre in the other was produced by the great Greek sculptor Phidias for
the temple at Olympus. That wooden statue of Zeus decorated with gold and
ivory was one of the wonders of the Ancient World. Sadly, we can judge it today
only from later marble copies.

The heyday of Ancient Roman sculpture came in the second and third centuries
A.D. and is associated with the sculpted portrait. The Hermitage collection, with
some 120 such likenesses, is considered one of the best in the world.

The decorative formality of the official commissioned portrait does not
obscure the subtle psychological characterization in the image of Lucius Verus,
who was co-ruler with Emperor Marcus Aurelius. The stamp of uncertainty
and anxiety lies on the plain, puffy face of Emperor Balbinus, who ruled briefly
in 238, and a coarse, masterful look to the portrait of the soldier-emperor
Philip the Arabian who came to power in the middle of the third century.
The last two date from the troubled period of decline that foreshadowed
the collapse of the Roman Empire.

A passageway created only in the twentieth century links the halls of
the New Hermitage with the Winter Palace. It has become a sort of bridge
connecting the Greek and Roman exhibits to the Ancient Egyptian collection.
The Hermitage's stock of artefacts from that very early centre of human
civilization is comparatively small, but the works in it — examples of monumental

*The Arrival of the First
Swallow Red-figure pelike
6th century B.C. Greece.
By Euphronios Earthenware*

Stele depicting Ipi, the pharaoh's major-domo and fan-bearer, before the god Anubis.
Memphis. First half of the 14th century B.C.

Amenemhat III
19th century B.C.
Middle Kingdom,
Ancient Egypt. Granite

In Ancient Egypt such monuments were set up in the tombs or temples of the pharaohs. Over the centuries their form changed extremely slowly — the pharaohs were depicted lither standing or seated with their hands laid on their knees. The face is a portrait: according to Ancient Egyptian beliefs a statue could become the dwelling place of a departed soul and a certain degree of likeness was therefore required.

Statuette. 15th century B.C.
Egypt. Wood

The male figure is depicted in the traditional pose — trunk straight, left leg advanced, arms down by the sides — but there is nothing forced about it. The characteristic features of the New Kingdom, last high point of Ancient Egyptian art — elegance and refinement — are present in full measure in this little masterpiece.

stone sculpture, small-scale plastic art, fragments of wall reliefs and papyruses, wood and stone sarcophagi, and mummies — give the visitor an idea of all the stages in the development of Ancient Egypt from its origins to its demise.

The Winter Palace houses one more unique collection, reliably protected in rooms with thick, windowless walls. This is the Hermitage's Golden Treasury. Kept here are works of precious metal and stone that belonged to peoples who once occupied the area of the northern Black Sea coast, the south of Russia, the Ukraine, the Caucasus and the Urals — the nomadic Scythians, Sarmatians and Khazars, and representatives of two great ancient civilisations, Greeks

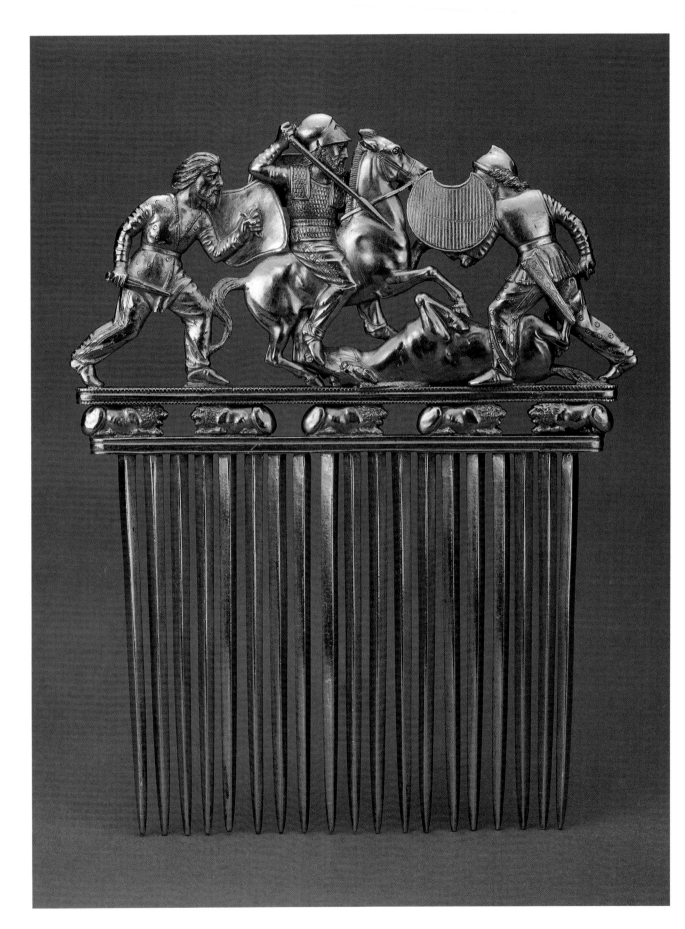

and Romans. Here too are items of jewellery, vessels and weapons from the lands of the East. The burial mounds of the Scythian nobility have yielded fabulous riches: magnificent works of gold and silver produced at the end of the first millennium B.C. The golden deer depicted in headlong flight by the craftsman is believed to have served as a boss for a warrior's shield. It is one of the masterpieces of the Scythian "Animal Style". The deer was evidently venerated as one of the main deities of the Scythians and therefore images of such beasts are particularly common in noble graves.

The Scythian burial mounds also produced superb examples of the Greek jeweller's art as rich chieftains often commissioned grave ornaments from

Diadem. 1st century A.D.
The Khokhlach burial
mound, known as the
"Novocherkassk Horde".
Gold, precious stones

This diadem found in a
Sarmatian grave is made up
of three connected sections.
In the centre is an ancient
cameo depicting a female
head.

Amphora. 4th century B.C.
Chermolyk burial mound.
Silver

This splendid example of
a Greek-made wine vessel
was found in a Scythian
grave close to the town
of Nikopol in the Ukraine.
All the gold relief-work that
adorns it strongly expresses
the world of Scythian
symbolism.

←
Comb. 4th century B.C.
Solokha burial mound. Gold

123

Small metal plaques from the Siberian Collection of Peter the Great. 4th–1st centuries B.C. Gold, turquoise

The Siberian Collection of Peter the Great was established on that Tsar's orders in 1715 and consisted of gold artefacts found in burial mounds in Siberia and the Altai mountains. The collection was displayed in the Kunstkammer (the museum Peter founded). The identity of the tribes who created these burial mounds is unknown, but the pieces of jewellery found there bear a strong resemblance to the Scythian Animal Style.

the skilled craftsmen who lived in the Greek city-colonies on the north coast of the Black Sea. The Solokha burial mound has given us the famous comb with fine proportions reminiscent of a Greek temple. The massive, four-sided teeth look like elegant columns supporting a frieze of lions that seem to bend beneath the weight of fighting warriors in Scythian dress who are entwined in a manner that looks like the pediment of the temple.

The Chertomlyk burial mound rendered a splendid silver amphora (a Greek wine vessel) decorated with reliefs that draw heavily on Scythian symbolism. On the shoulders of the vase we find winged griffins attacking a deer — one of the standard motifs of the Animal Style; below is a highly expressive scene of Scythians taming horses. The central spigot for drawing the wine is the head of a winged horse, while the two side ones are in the shape of lion's heads. The body of the vessel is covered with stylised ornament in the form of birds and plants. True masterpieces of Greek jewellery were found in the Kul-Oba mound near Kerch, which, as Pantikapaion, was capital of the ancient Bosporan kingdom. Testimony to the skills of a Greek craftsman who seems to have known all the secrets of his art are a priceless set of pendants designed to be worn at the temples. They consist of a large gold disc bearing the head of Athene, the goddess of wisdom, and a host of tiny amphorae suspended from it by extremely fine gold threads.

Another special treasury contains unique items by Western European craftsmen that from the eighteenth century up to the revolution were in the imperial family's Jewellery Gallery. Working to commissions from Empresses Anna, Elizabeth and, especially, Catherine the Great, the finest jewellers in Europe and the court jewellers Pausier and Duval produced snuff-boxes and

Deer. 7th–6th century B.C. Burial mound by the Cossack settlement of Kostromskaya. Gold

*Temple pendant bearing
the head of Athene.
4th century B.C. Kul-Oba
burial mound. Gold*

In 1830 soldiers cutting
stone on the slope of a
mountain near Kerch came
across an extremely rich
tomb of Greek origin in
which a noble Bosporan,
his wife and a slave armour-
bearer were buried. Among
the many first-rate items
of jewellery found at this site
were these superb elements
of a woman's head-dress.

holders for beauty-spots, necklaces and earrings, pendants and bouquets spangled with diamonds, emeralds, sapphires and rubies to amuse and adorn their crowned patrons. The Great Crown that Pausier created for Catherine was, in his own

Box for beauty spots bearing the monogram of Empress Elizabeth. Late 1740s. Jeweller J. Pausier(?). Gold, diamonds

Such small, flat containers with a mirror inside the lid were an essential fashion accessory for a society lady of the mid-18th century. They were used to keep artificial moles of black taffeta, velvet or paper which women applied to their faces, necks or breasts when attending balls and public functions. A beauty spot could be used to disguise some imperfection on the skin, but more often it had another purpose. At that time there was even a special, highly explicit language of beauty spots, that was, however, known only to the initiated. A spot in the middle of the forehead, for example, suggested "majesty"; one at the corner of the eye "passion"; one near a dimple on the cheek "jollity"; one on the lip "coquetry". At a ball particularly practised ladies would use the mirror to swiftly change the position of their beauty spots, thus revealing their secret desires to their chosen partner.

Bouquet of precious stones in a glass vessel. Late 1750s. Jeweller Louis David Duval

In the centre is a huge amethyst, superbly worked into the form of a tulip, surrounded with the tiniest cut diamonds. Emeralds, rubies, Dutch topazes, pyropes, spinel, aquamarines and turquoises were also used to make this bouquet.

words, the costliest thing existing in Europe. Today that gold crown, incorporating 5,000 diamonds and 75 pearls, is to be found, together with other items of imperial regalia, in the Diamond Fund in Moscow, but the Hermitage does possess unique miniature copies of the crown jewels produced by Carl Fabergé.

The Hermitage's numerous exhibits, peacefully coexisting in the one museum, serve as a vivid illustration of the fascinating complexity of the world's cultural history.

Foreword by Mikhail Piotrovksy
Introduction by Vladimir Matveyev
Text and compilation by Sergei Vesnin,
Sophia Kudriavtseva, Tatiana Pashkova
English translation by Paul Williams
Designed by Nikolai Kutovoy
Colour correction by Liubov Kornilova
Computer type-setting by Yelena Morozova
Photographs by Darya Bobrova, Leonid Bogdanov, Pavel Demidov,
Alexander Gronsky, Sergei Falin, Leonard Kheifets,
Victor Savik, Georgy Shablovsky, Vladimir Terebin, Oleg Trubsky
Edited by Maria Lyzhenkova
Managing Editor Nina Grishina

Printed and bound by the Ivan Fiodorov Printing Company, St Petersburg (No 7919)